The Schoolie

Observations on Life through the Window of a School Bus

Suzanne Cruz

En Route Books and Media, LLC
St. Louis, MO

Make the time

En Route Books and Media, LLC
5705 Rhodes Avenue
St. Louis, MO 63109

Cover credit: Sebastian Mahfood using DALL-E and author photos
Copyright © 2025 Suzanne Cruz

ISBN-13: 979-8-88870-458-5, 979-8-88870-526-1, & 979-8-88870-466-0
Library of Congress Control Number:
Available online at https://catalog.loc.gov

No part of this book may be reproduced, stored in a retrieval system, or transmitted in any form, or by any means, electronic, mechanical, photocopying, or otherwise, without the prior written permission of the author.

Table of Contents

Introduction 1

Chapter One: A Young Family 2

Chapter Two: Travel 34

Chapter Three: Innovation 65

Chapter Four: Playing with the Boys 88

Chapter Five: Jewels in Heaven 116

Chapter Six: Messes 143

Chapter Seven: Celebration 163

Chapter Eight: One door closes, One door opens 181

Introduction

Although Kennedy had been assassinated only a few years earlier, America still pulsed with a sense of optimism. The space race was soaring, gas was cheap, and big families packed up for the open road. It was the era of Camelot—when people still believed in possibility. Communities—local, familial, and national—were alive with energy, fueled by a post-war desire to build, explore, and connect. From 1970 to 1974, Americans gathered around their television sets to watch the Partridge Family roll from town to town in their rainbow-hued tour bus, singing songs of unity and freedom. Inspired by that same spirit, real families took to the highways in droves—some in recreational vehicles, others in hand-built camper shells, converted vans, or, like my parents, in a repurposed school bus. A "Schoolie"—equal parts grit and dream—became our family's ticket to roam.

Chapter One

A Young Family

Fidgeting with a greasy, broken carburetor at the kitchen table—because that's just where tools ended up—he looked up and said to mom, "Patsy, if you get pregnant one more time, we're going to have to buy a bus for all these kids." It sounded more like confusion than criticism, as if he still hadn't quite figured out how it kept happening. The smell of spaghetti drifted in from the kitchen—warm, familiar, and a little too garlicky—adding to the everyday chaos. Not long after, Mom's growing belly quietly confirmed baby number eight was on the way. And sure enough, true to his word, he pulled up a week later to their house in San Leandro, California, driving a 1958 Ford school bus—yellow-orange, striped in black, and conveniently marked with a number eight.

"It's here, it's here!" Marc yelled. As the oldest of the five boys, he took his role seriously—part town crier, part junior foreman. He always seemed to know what was going on, even with a house full of noise and flying elbows. When I heard him shout, I came running, elbowed my way through the usual knot of siblings, and stopped short. I stared, wide-eyed, thinking, *Wow... Dad actually meant it.*

Looking past the bus, I noticed curtains twitching all down the street—neighbors peeking out like nosy extras in a play. If I had been a teenager, I probably would've ducked behind a bush in embarrassment. But I was still a kid, and honestly, I was proud. Nobody—*nobody*—had a school bus parked in their driveway. What we were about to witness over the next two years was nothing short of amazing: that big yellow bus slowly transforming into a camper, powered by nothing more than Dad's stubborn ingenuity and a lot of determination.

I'm still not sure whose idea it was to have so many kids—maybe it was hers, maybe the Pope's. Back then, that's just how it went in good Catholic families. But my mother did tell us stories about growing up lonely. Her only sibling, a younger sister, went to live with their father after my grandparents divorced when Mom was six—a real scandal at the time. Grandma found work as a secretary and enrolled Mom in Catholic school, where she had to stay with the nuns until five. Then she'd walk home, make dinner for herself and Grandma, who came through the door worn out from the day. It was just the two of them, quiet and tired. Mom used to say it was so quiet and lonely that you could hear the forks clanking on the plates in that small, empty house.

Mom always said she wanted a big family because the very idea of it just sounded… wonderful. The noise, the chaos, the endless swirl of activity—it lit her up. She thrived in the middle of it all, laughing easily, seeing the humor in life's messes. In fact, the bigger the mess, the harder she laughed. She was radiant in her own grounded way—short black hair, dark sparkling eyes full of mischief and kindness. A little on the round side and standing five foot four, always covered in food or baby slobber, yet, when it was time to go out the door, she pulled herself together. With a similar look of Liz Taylor, she was always composed, even when the world around her was anything but.

In her rare quiet moments, she was an artist. Watercolors, charcoal sketches, bits of collage—she saw beauty in the everyday and transformed it into something lasting. Her hands were just as quick with a paintbrush as they were folding laundry or soothing a crying child. That creative spirit was another thread in her tapestry of grace. People often wondered where her style came from—this woman married to a humble mechanic and a gaggle of kids always behind her. But that was Mom: full of surprises, full of joy, full of art, and full of heart. Above all, she loved being Catholic. She used to say there was something about being Catholic—the grandeur of cathedrals, the mystery of the Mass, the rhythm of the rituals. That reverence infused her whole being with elegance, like incense clinging to Sunday clothes.

She was proudly Portuguese, with roots as deep and salty as the Atlantic. Her father came from the Azores Islands—a speck of volcanic paradise in the middle of the sea—and in a bold stroke of youthful adventure, he crossed the ocean aboard a schooner. Not just any sailboat, mind you. No, she always called it a *schooner*, because that word alone felt like a breeze through history: romantic, windswept, and brave. Somewhere between the islands and America, he taught himself English—one word, one phrase at a time—listening to sailors swap stories and leafing through the only book he had packed: *Teach Yourself the English Language*. By the time he stepped ashore, he had a heart full of courage, a head full of new words, and the kind of grit that would shape generations to come.

Chapter One: A Young Family

And from him, she inherited not only dark eyes and sturdy pride, but that same adventurous spirit.

He eventually put down roots in Oakland, California, in the year 1898, a time when the West still felt like the edge of possibility. There, he opened a soda fountain saloon, a fine and proper establishment with a twist: one side for women and children, the other for men. That's just how the world worked back then sipping soda water on one side, gentlemen nursing something stronger on the other. Mom said it was a place of dignity and respect, where decorum mattered and so did good manners. Not long after, he met a lovely Portuguese Catholic woman, married her in true Old World fashion, and together they raised seven children. Her mother—my grandmother—was the eldest of the bunch.

Mom loved telling this story. She made sure we knew we came from strong stock—people with guts and grit, who crossed oceans in schooners and started businesses from scratch. It was her way of reminding us that determination ran in our blood—that whether it was a storm at sea or one of life's everyday squalls, we came from people who didn't just survive, they thrived.

Now Dad—well, his story was always a little more mysterious. I didn't know much, except for the whispered rumor that some distant male relative of his had murdered someone back in the old country and fled to America. Was it true? Who knows. But it sure made for a great campfire tale when the stars were out and the marshmallows were roasting. As for why *he* had so many kids? I doubt he had a grand plan. I think he just married his girlfriend—surprise!—she turned out to be a wife and mother. Or maybe, deep down, he liked the idea of being that legendary neighborhood figure: *"Hey, there goes that wild Italian-Catholic guy with the busload of kids!"*

Dad reminded me of Kirk Douglas in *Spartacus*—all strength and intensity, with that unmistakable Roman nose, a mop of fiery red hair, and piercing blue eyes. He had a barrel chest and a presence that filled the room. A heavy-duty mechanic, no matter how many showers he took after work, Dad always carried with him the faint, lingering scent of diesel grease. It clung to him like a second skin—part cologne, part calling card. He was the kind of tradesman who could take apart an engine blindfolded and put it back together before dinner. That smell, mixed with the grit under his nails and the creases in his hands, became part of his signature—proof of a man who worked hard, got dirty, and never once complained. But what I remember most were his hands. Hands of steel. Worn from a lifetime under the hood of cars—grease-stained, nails chipped, skin cracked like old leather. I'd stare at them sometimes, those quiet, hardworking hands, and feel a tenderness. They told a story of sacrifice, grit, and a kind of silent love that didn't need words to be real.

And so, this great big family learned by doing—shoulder to shoulder with their dad, tearing things apart, putting them back together, designing as they went. From him, we picked up grit, ingenuity, and the art of creative problem-solving with whatever was on hand. From Mom, we learned patience, love, and the quiet power of tolerance, all with her good sense of style—usually served with a side of laughter so strong it could melt tension like butter on toast.

Chapter One: A Young Family

When Dad brought home the bus, life shifted into a whole new gear. That old yellow school bus parked in our yard became the family project, the family dream. First came the demolition: seats ripped out and tossed into a towering green mountain on the front lawn—so high my seven-year-old eyes couldn't see over it. Then, piece by piece, came the makings of our new home-on-wheels. A 55-gallon oil drum, perfect (according to Dad) for a septic tank. Pipes—copper, PVC, it didn't matter—collected from work or bartered for in some backlot handshake. A massive battery from a Caterpillar bulldozer was tucked under a storage cabinet like buried treasure. Propane tanks, wires, switches, everything mounted with purpose and a touch of mad genius beneath the belly of the bus.

There was a water pump from the local camper supply store, and a toilet gifted (or maybe traded?) from that guy who had the horses—you know the one, always up for a deal. Square recessed lights were scored from a dusty supply shop, and steel piping, rescued from the scrap pile at Dad's work yard, was transformed into a sturdy ladder bolted to the back of the bus. And that ladder? It didn't just lead somewhere practical—it led to magic. At the top, Dad built a plywood platform strong enough for folding chairs, kids, and blankets. From up there, we watched parades like royalty, waving at marching bands and floats from our homemade rooftop grandstand. It wasn't just a bus. It was our castle on wheels.

Painting the exterior of the bus was no rushed affair—it was done with steady hands, great patience, and quiet pride. I remember watching Dad, mesmerized by the rhythmic motion of his arm as he glided the paint sprayer back and forth. He never lingered, releasing the trigger with precision at the end of each sweep to avoid drips. I didn't ask questions. I just sat there in silence, soaking in the lesson—the kind you don't get from words.

While their friends lobbied for psychedelic colors or wild designs, my parents stayed true to their own vision. They chose a warm, comforting tan for the body and a rich root beer brown band that wrapped around the length like a gentle hug. It was tasteful, classic, a little nostalgic. And then, Dad found an old Volkswagen emblem in the local wrecking yard and proudly mounted it on the front. Just to mess with people. And it worked—because nothing confused folks more than a giant tan bus with eight kids inside proudly sporting the badge of a Beetle.

Once the inside and outside of the bus were nearly finished, Dad dove headfirst into what may have been his favorite part: the engine. He installed a souped-up 292 V8, paired with a 4-speed transmission and a two-speed rear end—because hauling that kind of weight across countless miles wasn't a job for amateurs. It was a mission, and it needed a mechanic behind the wheel and under the hood.

If you wanted time with Dad, you had to earn it—in the garage. That was his sanctuary, his classroom, and his workshop all in one. The moment you stepped in, he handed you a wrench, a rag, or a wire and turned it into a learning opportunity. You never really saw all of him—just his legs sticking out from under the engine, or his feet poking out as the rest of him disappeared beneath the bus on that little rolling board we called a crawler. Occasionally, his face would pop into view—smudged with grease, sweat, and a glint of satisfaction in his eyes. It was in those gritty, oily moments that I saw what real work looked like—and what quiet love looked like, too.

Once I did get Dad's attention, I usually ended up with the same faithful jobs—sliding heavy blocks behind the giant tires of the bus, handing him socket wrenches, flathead screwdrivers, or pliers, and sometimes just running to get his coffee. But I was there. And that mattered. Being in his orbit meant absorbing his quiet reverence for things well-built, for tools and machines that had a purpose and a soul.

His toolboxes were works of art: everything in its place, clean, cared for, respected. To him, tools weren't just objects, they were lifelines. Good tools meant transportation. Transportation meant work. And work meant survival, dignity, and providing for a family. Take care of your tools, he'd say without saying it, and they'll take care of you. That lesson—unspoken, yet crystal clear—stayed with me the rest of my life.

Late one night, long after dinner had turned into legend, I stood waiting for my next order, bored stiff, when I locked eyes with a giant bottle of orange pumice soap perched like a crown jewel on the edge of Dad's workbench. It practically dared me to press its pump—seducing me with its thick, swirly promise of citrus-scented mischief. I knew better. That stuff was meant for scrubbing off the kind of industrial filth Dad collected like badges of honor—diesel grease, axle grime, the kind of grit that made your skin look paved. But I spotted one lone smudge of grease on my thumb, and that was justification enough. One satisfying squirt later, I had a generous glob oozing into my palm. I rubbed it luxuriously between my fingers, hypnotized by the gooey orange lava lamp I was creating. I was mid-transcendental goop meditation when Dad's voice cut through the silence like a wrench to the floor—

"Becca, go get me that wrench, quick".

"Crap." I grabbed the quickest thing I could find, his shirt, and wiped it off.

"Here dad, here's the wrench".

"Thanks", came the voice from under the bus.

"Well, I gotta go now dad."

Sprinting across the sprawling backyard, tangled with weeds and wild grass, a sharp shout ripped through the air from the garage. "What the heck?" Heart pounding, momentum carried me across the yard and safely inside.

Late at night, exhausted from work and his many duties, dad turned on the TV and settled down on his recliner. "Becca," he called from the front room.

"Yea, Daddy?"

"Go get your dad a beer."

"Ok," I walked to the kitchen as the familiar song drifted into the hall,

"…boys were boys and men were men; mister we could use a man like Herbert Hoover again. Gee our ol' LaSalle ran great, those were the days."

Archie Bunker was on, mom sat next to dad on the couch, and they settled into the world of TV land as they howled, "Meat Head, let me tell you……" by the time I brought dad his beer he was already snoring.

Chapter One: A Young Family

Marc, my oldest brother took after my dad, as he watched dad build and redesign, it inspired him to do the same with all his toys. That is how we all learned. Someone always had something pulled apart. One time mom came looking for her diamond watch and found it in pieces on my brother Paul's desk next to a pair of needle nose pliers. Paul, I think, had ADD or ADHD; in either case all I know is that he always in trouble and had to take a daily pill for it. He was teased mercilessly for it.

"Paul, Paul, time for your pill; you can't sit still, you never will!"

Searching for my trusty tricycle one day, I realized it had vanished. Or so I thought. There it was, hiding in the garage, though barely recognizable. Marc had flipped the frame upside down, transforming it into a sleek, low-riding machine. It looked like something a tiny Mexican low-rider might cruise down the driveway in. Surprisingly, it was a blast to ride—legs stretched out, arms wide, like you were in some kind of mini dragster. To this day, I swear someone must've seen that thing, because not long after, the plastic Big Wheel hit the shelves. Coincidence? I think not.

Summer meant freedom. Once school let out, we gave ourselves over completely to the outdoors. Ideas—born of boredom or pure necessity—poured in like sunshine. Our bikes became our most prized possessions, as sacred to us as any car to a grown-up. They meant speed, escape, and the thrill of independence. Marc built ramps out of scrap wood, and we'd launch ourselves into the air, daring gravity to catch us. In those wild moments, as we pushed our bikes—and ourselves—to the edge, we discovered what courage felt like, one scraped elbow at a time.

One golden summer afternoon, Marc called out for volunteers, his latest invention was ready for its test run. He had rigged our red wagon to the back of his 10-speed bike with the precision of a teenage genius. At just sixteen, he was already a wizard with an arc welder and had welded the wagon's arm so it stayed stiff, no more wobbling up and down. He secured the handle under his bike seat with a length of rope and shouted, "Who wants a ride?"

I trusted Marc with the blind loyalty only a younger sibling can muster. I climbed in without hesitation and convinced my little brother Vincent to join me. Ever the cautious engineer, Marc handed us each a baseball cap—his idea of safety gear—and off we went.

The cul-de-sac out front was the perfect proving ground. We circled slowly at first, laughter bubbling up as the wheels found their rhythm. Then I shouted, "Winecha go faster, Marc?"—and just like that, we were flying. The wind whipped past our faces, our grins stretched wide. What a ride it was—part rollercoaster, part rocket launch, and all the magic of childhood in motion.

Suddenly, I heard a sound like a cat's howl—only to realize it was me, yowling as my body tumbled out of the wagon. I rolled a good three times before coming to a stop, winded, with Vincent's leg draped across my throat. For a moment, I gasped for air like a fish on a dock. Then Vincent was up and gone—skinned elbows, bloody knees—sprinting into the house in a blur of panic and tears.

I wanted to cry, too. My lip quivered, but I clenched my jaw and told myself that saints didn't cry. So, I didn't. Marc looked horrified. I waved him off and said I was fine; told him I was tough. And I believed it—at least for a while.

Chapter One: A Young Family

It wasn't until much later in life that I learned toughness has two sides. There's the kind that builds you up, and the kind that grinds you down. There's blind, stubborn suffering, and then there's suffering that forges you. History tends to remember the strongest souls as the ones marked with scars—not because they never fell, but because they kept getting back up.

Aside from Marc and his crazy inventions, one of the other best things about growing up in a big family was never being without an ally. If one sibling annoyed you, you just moved on to the next and asked, "Hey, wanna play?" And as one of the youngest, there was always an older lap to crawl into when the world felt heavy.

What I was most proud of wasn't a shiny bike or the latest toy—it was my brothers. All five of them. It felt like I had my own personal security detail, a full-time squad of muscle in hand-me-down jeans. At school, if someone so much as looked at me sideways, I'd raise my tiny hand, fingers spread wide, and deliver the line with quiet confidence: "Back off—or my five brothers will rearrange your face."

That usually did the trick. A nearby kid would lean in and whisper, "Careful, she does have five brothers." And just like that, the situation was defused. No fights, no fuss, just the unspoken magic of having an army in your corner—and the wisdom to weaponize it with flair.

There was a price to pay for all that brotherly protection: I had to fit in. And fitting in with boys meant mastering their strange, sacred code—something they called funny. It wasn't enough to just be smart or quick; you had to be a smart-ass, armed with wit, timing, and an unspoken agreement that everything—everything—was fair game if it got a laugh.

My first attempt at cracking this elusive code happened at the San Diego Zoo. Our family—this lumbering parade of kids and parents—wandered into the fowl exhibit. Turkeys strutted. Game hens clucked. Then we all paused in front of one particularly glorious chicken, puffed up like royalty in full feather.

This was my moment.

"Hey Marc," I said, loud enough for full comedic impact. "See that chicken? I'm gonna eat the next thing that comes outta its butt."

There was a sharp gasp. Not from my audience—no, they were already breaking into grins, but from my mom. Then came the slap. Right across the mouth.

That's when I learned there's a second golden rule to comedy: always check who's within earshot.

I rubbed my stinging lip and glanced around, hoping the joke had landed. It had. My brothers were doubled over, wheezing with laughter. At the time, I wasn't sure if they thought the line was actually funny—or if they were just impressed I'd been bold (or dumb) enough to say it in front of Mom.

Years later, I've figured it out: it was the latter.

The first Earth Day rolled around in April of 1970, and like many well-meaning Americans, Mom and Dad decided to do their part by starting a victory garden. Our days were soon filled with the rumble of the Rototiller and fragrant family outings to nearby farms to collect manure, bucket after ripe, steamy bucket—for our

Chapter One: A Young Family

growing mulch pile. Eggshells, banana peels, coffee grounds, anything vaguely biodegradable went in.

Biodegradable. I loved that word. I loved knowing what it meant and being able to pronounce it like a tenured professor. As kids often do, I absorbed the latest family obsession and made it my whole identity: I became Organic Gardening Girl.

My big debut came during science class. I spotted a banana peel in my lunch bag and noticed the patch of dirt just outside the classroom window. It was fate. With bold confidence, I launched the peel out the window like some eco-conscious revolutionary. The mean girls' table gasped in unison. "Eww! She's littering!" I turned, cool as compost, and delivered the line with smug precision:

"Hey. It's biodegradable."

"What does that even mean?" they snapped.

I just smiled, grabbed my milk carton, and walked off like I had dirt under my fingernails and secrets in my soil. Let them stew in their cafeteria plastic and ignorance. Mean girls, they act like they know everything, until you throw a banana at science.

Our family victory garden stretched across half an acre, with winding dirt paths cut between squares of corn, artichokes, squash, fruit trees, and tidy rows of smaller plants—lettuce, onions, tomatoes. Our job was weeding, though distinguishing weeds from vegetables wasn't an exact science. The method was simple: pull it. If it came out too easily, oops—that was a vegetable.

The next morning, our mistakes were obvious. Wilted, slumped-over plants stood like sad little reminders of our agricultural crimes. But weeds were not the only problem, pests of every kind came to have a bite out of our garden. Dad read his subscription of "Organic Gardening" like the bible, and its message was clear: the healthier the crop, the fewer pests you'd have. However, although dad repeated the gospel, I wasn't convinced. I loved artichokes, but unfortunately, so did earwigs. Drop a fresh-picked artichoke into boiling water and out floated the earwigs like they were enjoying a spa day. Eeww.

What we did not grow, we went to the store for, simply going to the store was a high-risk operation for a woman with so many kids. Someone almost always got forgotten, usually because Blaise thought it was hilarious to keep shifting places in line, throwing off the count. "One, two, three, four, five, six, seven, eight—good, they're all here!" she'd announce with the efficiency of a drill sergeant. Maybe, just maybe, I am thinking, Mom "accidentally-on-purpose" left one of us behind now and then to teach us a little independence. Her motto was clear:

"I'm not raising children. I'm raising adults."

And honestly? That's a solid point. Kids don't grow up to be bigger kids; they grow up to be adults. And an adult, in her book, was someone responsible, respectful, and able to figure things out for themselves, or at least how to find the answer. Getting lost in a store, as it turned out, was just another part of the curriculum.

It was thanks to all these little gems of wisdom floating around our house that I became an avid note-taker. I was never without a composition book, often receiving a fresh one for Christmas or my birthday, right alongside the socks and shampoo.

To be fair, there were plenty of crossed-out insights on those pages. Like the time I realized Mom's relentless push for independence in her children wasn't just about building character—it was

Chapter One: A Young Family

also about buying herself five minutes to sip her coffee and take a Midol. Genius, really. She kept the bottle tucked in the pocket of her robe, a quiet act of self-preservation amid the chaos of eight children.

But you'd never know how tired she was when she walked out the front door, once she stepped outside, she was composed, polished, and put-together. Where did she learn this? Maybe it was all those afternoons spent with the nuns as a child, or maybe it was her mother's Portuguese elegance, but wherever it came from, I noticed. Her hair was always perfectly coiffed, a fresh swipe of lipstick never far from her smile. Her outfits were simple, coordinated, and somehow always effortlessly chic—like she'd just stepped out of a magazine for modest moms with impeccable taste. If any of us dared to sneak out looking rumpled or wild-haired, a voice would thunder from the ether:

"Stop! Don't you dare leave this house looking like that!"

Before you could blink, an arm would appear—like a stylish guardian angel—yanking you back inside, slapping a sun hat on your head, and smoothing your shirt with military precision. Only after modest clothing was straightened, hair was brushed, and a respectable smile was plastered on our face were we cleared for public appearance. "You get treated with respect when you respect yourself," she'd always say, her mantra, and our unofficial uniform code.

And that made perfect sense to me. So, I wrote it down.

On the rare occasion Mom left the house alone, there was no telling when she'd be back—or when we'd eat again. But that was okay. We were resourceful. We had a Victory Garden! Lunch was straightforward: grab a knife from the kitchen, march out back, and find the perfect summer squash. Whack it off at the stem like a pioneer on a mission. Then drag a chair over to the stove, fill a pot with water, and bring it to a boil. In goes the squash. Wait until it's soft, drain the water, plop it in a bowl, drown it in half a pound of butter, sprinkle on some salt, and voilà—full tummy, crisis averted.

My older brother Blaise had more ambitious tastes. One day, he struck gold in the fridge and found some fresh ground beef from the butcher. Jackpot. He tore it open, rolled the meat into little balls with his hands, speared one on a fork, and fired up the electric burner. Then, like a miniature caveman chef, he began slow roasting it over the coils. A dash of Mrs. Dash for flair. When it started to snap and sizzle, he declared it done. He gave it a quick blow, took a bite, and let out a satisfied sigh, as if he'd just cooked a five-star meal.

My little brother Vincent and I watched in awe—and, frankly, in jealousy. Why were we stuck eating vegetables when we could have meat? Determined to level up, I followed Blaise's method to the letter. I rolled my own meatballs, skewered one on a fork, cooked it to perfection, and proudly offered the first bite to Vincent. His big brown eyes sparkled; his mouth, already open and drooling in anticipation. I handed it to him—and only then realized I hadn't blown on the fork. He bit down. Right onto the scalding metal. Too late. The poor kid had fork marks branded on his lips for a week. No amount of ice—or apologies—could undo that mistake. Rule of thumb: you always, always fed the younger ones before yourself. Which meant Little Andy never had to cook a thing. Ever. But Vincent, nursing his blistered lips, looked over at him and said, "You know, Andy... there is the safety benefit of learning to cook for yourself."

One fine spring day, Dad was outside, crouched next to the bus, welding a hinge onto the side storage compartment. I wandered by—eight years old, a red licorice rope dangling from my mouth like a lazy ribbon, sticky juice dribbling down my chin. Without even looking up, Dad reached out, wiped it away with his work-worn hand—and smeared it straight onto his pants. "Becca," he said, brushing off his jeans with a shrug, "I'm done. We're ready to travel."

With a satisfying clang, he dropped the compartment door shut. It clicked perfectly into place, like everything was finally in order.

Bang! The starting gun fired, and I was yanked out of my daydream and off the blocks in a heartbeat. Track was the perfect high school sport—if you had no other talents, you could just run. Simple. At the far end of the track stood a row of giant oak trees, their leaves trembling gently in the breeze. It was a warm spring afternoon; the kind of day that made you feel like anything was possible. And I was fast. Way ahead of the other girls, my head down, my mind locked in. Until I caught sight of them—the boys loitering at the sideline. They weren't there for the race. They were there for the view. Then I heard one of them say, clear as day:

"That girl's got a cute ass." My heart flared with fury. The disrespect, the arrogance. But as I rounded the curve, something strange happened. I caught myself gawking at the one who said it. That split-second glance cost me. I lost my rhythm. I lost my lead. I crossed the finish line in third place, teeth clenched with rage—not at him, but at myself. I scolded myself, "You idiot, keep your mind on the race!"

I jogged off to the shade by the restrooms to cool down and catch my breath. And just as I'd predicted—here he came. That swagger, that stupid smirk. Probably ready to offer condolences… or worse, some unsolicited advice.

"Hey," he said, flashing a grin like he'd practiced it in the mirror. "I'm Lorenzo. I noticed you run with your arms kind of out." Here it comes, I thought. "If you keep them in, closer to your body," he continued, "you might find you can go a little faster."

I forced a smile. "Geez, thanks," I said, trying to sound civil. Inwardly, I was seething. Yeah, buddy—maybe if you hadn't been standing at the side of the track making comments about girls' asses and being a walking distraction, I might've run faster, too. Jerk. I told him my name, tossed out a half-hearted, surly "thank you," and then didn't say another word.

And so, as the insanity of life would prove itself again, we had lunch together every day after that and became inseparable, he seventeen and me sixteen. He laughed easily and was big and strong. He told me he was of Spanish descent but later admitted to being half El Salvadorian. He told me that he thought saying he was Spanish was more mysterious. That was a big deal to him, being mysterious! Lorenzo was tall, about six-foot, two inches, and he made an impressive figure, enough to be intimidating to bullies, so many made him his friend. But teachers liked him, too. Once, I saw

Chapter One: A Young Family

coach Smith stride across the football field seek him out, put his arm around his back, and motion for him to take the rest of the guys out for a run. He was likable with a keen wit and compassion for others. His flirtatious mannerisms made him a hit with the females, too.

Although I first met him at a track meet, Lorenzo's real passion was football. His parents showed up to every game, and you could see his dad yelling and screaming so hard his veins popped out of his forehead. At first, I figured he was just a loving father who also loved football. But when I was introduced to the family, their "welcome" came with a side of unsolicited advice—like dropping my Catholicism to become Protestant, not aiming too high in life, and how to be a good servant to their son. Their suggestions for me—and their criticisms of Lorenzo—never seemed to stop. Lorenzo was expected to attend every football practice, every weekend workshop, and certainly every game. His father told me with pride that Lorenzo would be the next Joe Namath. When that happened, he could quit his job as a prison guard.

"Lorenzo is my retirement plan," he boasted.

At sixteen, I had no idea what that meant—but it sounded… okay. Kinda, I guess.

For some other strange reason, we became a high-school couple. Lorenzo felt that now that he had a woman, his life was complete. I did not really share his sense of accomplishment. It seemed to me that there were a whole-heck-of-a-lot of other options out there in the big wide world other than getting a girl. I mean once you get a girl, she is just going to want stuff, a home, a car, a family, financial security. Didn't he want to go out into the world and slay life's dragons? I voiced my question to him, and he brushed me off; that should have been a clue. But we Catholics, I think, are a little co-dependent by training, always seeking ways to help others see the best in themselves or point to open doors when they could care less. Everyone in high school had a boyfriend or girlfriend; you just did, so you would fit in. And it was better to choose one rather than have one chosen for you. And once you had a "steady," all your friends would say, "Oh, you're such a cute couple!" What the heck, I'm only sixteen! But that does not matter to tribes of teens and God forbid if you want to break up! Which we did, often!

"Oh, my Gowd, you broke up with Lorenzo? You were so perfect for each other!" "But I'm only sixteen," I would protest!

If you think about it, the word friend is right there at the end of boyfriend or girlfriend—which should mean it's someone you can confide in. Lorenzo needed someone to talk to, and I was a good listener. It made sense. He told me about the night his dad came home drunk and picked a fight with him over some tools left outside. Then he stumbled off to bed, only to be heard yelling at his wife after she brought him dinner:

"Maria! You forgot the hot sauce!"

Then Maria—his mom—would go running like a linebacker, shoving her smaller children out of the way to meet his every tiny, stupid demand. It made Lorenzo furious. He loved his mom and hated watching her bow to his dad. He wished, more than anything, that she'd stand up for herself.

Sometimes, I'd tell Lorenzo what it was like living with my genius, building brothers, my dad, and the bus. He didn't believe me at first—he couldn't. He came from a world where nothing was built, only torn down. In his football-obsessed family, it was all crash, bang, and domination. But the day I brought him over and he saw that school bus conversion parked in our yard, something shifted. He became a believer. He realized there were families that created instead of destroyed—families that built each other up rather than tore each other down with criticism and control. Who knows when a young person's image of themselves becomes too cracked to repair. I didn't see it at the time. But my mother—who liked Lorenzo well enough—suspected early on that this relationship between the builder and the breaker was bound to end in rubble.

Often, we lay underneath the shade of a tree and share our dreams and accomplishments. He would often speak of his Little League Wins, Pop Waner Football championships, and High School sports. I would share my dream of going to college and becoming something. Lorenzo heard, but he did not listen. This was weird. Didn't this guy think about what he wanted to do when he grew up? The things we talked about never really meshed up, and we argued a lot. But youth makes for kindred spirits, and when you are young you think it is enough to have laughter and love in common; trust me, it is not. Because when you are young, there is so much time. We drove for long drives and watched the sunsets. We were not passionate about world affairs. We were just in awe of the world and its possibilities, and, hey, we both liked pizza, and that seemed to be enough.

Sitting in the front room with my mom one Saturday afternoon, we heard car tires screech and a horn honk. I hurdled over the couch, grabbed my bag on the table and headed for the door, only to have my arm grabbed by that stylish Guardian Angel.

"Every time he honks the horn, you go running. Stop. Have some class." Those words from my mom stuck. And I thought, "Ya know what, Mom? You're right." So that day, I didn't dash out the door—I sauntered. Like a real classy lady. And I made him wait. He had come in his new car. A beater of a Chevy Impala. The vinyl roof had long since peeled off, leaving the top rusted raw. The rest of the body was white—well, mostly—scratched and speckled with a kind of accidental rust mosaic. It got two gallons to the mile, and he was forever stopping to fill it up. The passenger door didn't open, so I climbed in through the open window, legs first, like I was sneaking into my own bad decision.

Lorenzo flashed a big grin. "We," he said, "are going to the lake."

It was only a 25-minute drive to the lake. Once we got there, he pulled the car up close to the bank—muddy and soft from recent rain. Being the daughter of a mechanic, I was fluent in car-speak. I could change the oil by age ten, and by eleven I was driving a stick shift around back roads. But that knowledge came with a dilemma: girls weren't supposed to tell guys how to drive. It came off as bossy, or worse, like you were trying to one-up them. So, I watched in silence as the front tires sank slightly into the mud. All I allowed myself to say was, "Aaaahhh... I don't think that's a good idea."

"It's fine," he said, puffing out his chest like a Boy Scout who'd just earned a badge in Overconfidence. "Come on, let's go swimming."

Chapter One: A Young Family

I didn't argue—better to seem agreeable than difficult—so I shrugged and let it go. Still, my brain was doing somersaults trying to process the idea of a nearly grown man who clearly had no idea what he was doing. It was like watching someone confidently assemble boxed furniture with a butter knife.

It was August, and the water was warm that time of year. The reservoir stretched so wide you could spend an entire day swimming and not see another soul despite the fact that everyone in our little mountain town practically lived near the water in the summer. The cool water was refreshing, and no sooner had I jumped in than I felt my swimsuit yanked clean off. Lorenzo popped up a few feet away, grinning like a fool, holding my suit high above the water like some victorious Indian warrior who had just counted coup. Holy crap—I'm naked. Skinny dipping. This is it. I'd heard of such things, but in my mind, that was what bad girls did. I was done for.

"Lorenzo!" I shouted, panicked. "I'm going to hell. You don't want me to go to hell, do you? Give me back my suit!"

His response? Singing "Only the Good Die Young" by Billy Joel, full voice and out of tune. Hopeless.

"Lorenzo, knock it off. It's not funny anymore. Stop," I pleaded.

Eventually, he relented and handed it back—still laughing, of course.

As the sun dipped low and the air cooled, we made our way back to the car—only to find his beloved Chevy Impala's tires now sunk a few extra inches into the mud. We stared at the wheels, then at each other.

"Go ahead and get in," he said, all confidence. "I got this handled."

Ohhh boy. Suuuure you do, I thought. I climbed in anyway, bracing myself for the inevitable. He fired up the engine and, instead of gently coaxing the car free, floored it like we were drag racing at Daytona. The tires spun, spat mud, and sank deeper. We were now officially stuck. And me? I'm proud to say that I resisted every ounce of temptation to say, "I told you so." (Though I may have thought it very loudly.)

"Fuuuuuuck," came his response, long and dramatic. Drive. Reverse. Drive. Reverse. Drive. Reverse. After a few rounds of this muddy dance, he turned to me and said, "You drive—I'll push." Fine by me. I've always believed it's better to show people than to tell them. Some lessons stick better when they come with a little splatter. So, I slid behind the wheel and eased onto the gas. "Give it a little more!" Lorenzo shouted from behind. I didn't agree, but I did it anyway. The tires spun, mud flew—and absolutely pelted him. "Fuuuuuuck!" he screamed again, now with much more feeling.

By the time the sun set—and sixty bucks had been handed over to the tow truck guy—we made it back to Lorenzo's house. His mom was already at the door.

"Why are you late? And why are you covered in mud?"

As we trudged up the stairs to the kitchen, he launched into the story. The Galloping Gourmet was on the TV—rabbit ears wrapped in tinfoil, the picture a snowy blur. Lorenzo's sister sat inches from the screen, fully locked in and squinting to make out Graham Kerr, who was grinning wildly while dumping sizzling bacon grease over vegetables like he'd discovered fire. Wine in hand, of course. Lorenzo took his usual spot at the kitchen table while his mom stood nearby, half-listening. I stood off to the side, trying not to stare at the cigarette dangling from her lips—held there, quite impressively, by a crusty dot of dried saliva. She was nothing like my mom.

"Hmm. Alright," she finally said. "Take your girlfriend home, then get right back here. You hear me?"

That day at the lake, Lorenzo learned that with the freedom of owning a Chevy came responsibility—but not the kind you'd expect. No, for him it was the art of not getting caught. Most people mess up, file the experience under "Life Lessons," and move on a little wiser. Lorenzo? Not so much. His takeaway was more like, "Well, that didn't work. Next time, I just need a better cover story."

By summer's end, Lorenzo had graduated high school and taken a job as a seasonal firefighter. Our high school romance, like the season itself, had burned hot, fizzled fast, and ended without ceremony.

Senior year crept in, and with it came a heavy wave of depression. While my friends buzzed with excitement over college applications and campus tours, I knew that road wasn't mine to take. My parents had a firm philosophy: once you hit eighteen, you're out. Here's your suitcase, kid. Good luck, God bless, and don't let the door hit you on the way out. All sarcasm aside, with so many mouths to feed, college was never in the cards unless we figured it out ourselves. My parents had only finished high school and were completely in the dark when it came to college applications, scholarships, or anything beyond a guidance counselor's door. And in our family—as in many big families—there was always some fresh crisis gobbling up attention and resources. If it wasn't a hospital bill, it was a broken-down car, or a sibling going off the rails. Stability was elusive. To make things even more chaotic, my parents had a habit of moving. Constantly. I'm still not entirely sure why. Maybe it was Dad's job—he'd get called to new construction sites where his mechanical know-how was needed. Or maybe, after four years in a town, they'd look at each other and say, "Welp, time to sell the house, pack up whoever's still living with us, and go see how the sun sets somewhere else."

My senior year, I wandered the school halls in a daze of hormonal angst. Like most teenage girls, I couldn't help but compare. The other girls floated past in trendy outfits, arms linked with besties, whispering their college choices like they were state secrets. They clutched their binders and Texas Instrument calculators like golden tickets to a promising future. I, on the other hand, clutched my jealousy and low-grade Catholic guilt. It all felt so unfair. The Church's best offering? A vague reassurance that suffering was redemptive—as if that would pair well with cafeteria meatloaf and a C in Algebra II. I was supposed to believe my pain had purpose, while everyone else was packing for dorm life and careers that promised both money and matching pantsuits.

Then one day in History class, we watched a documentary about Eleanor Roosevelt. The narrator intoned, "It was at Finishing School where Eleanor finally came into her own." And all I could think was, "Well, how delightful for Eleanor and her magical Finishing School." Meanwhile, I was staring down the barrel of the great and terrifying unknown—with nothing but sarcasm and a rosary to guide me.

Graduation came and went with little fanfare. I was the oldest still at home now—just Andy and me left from the group Mom used to call "The Three Little Ones." Vince had already taken off for the seminary the year before, where he began dazzling everyone within a hundred-mile radius. At one point, he was even sent to Guam to help prepare for Pope John Paul II's visit. Guam! For the Pope! Mom practically floated through town with pride, stopping unsuspecting neighbors mid-errand to deliver unsolicited updates. She made sure the grocery store checkout line got the Vatican report whether they asked for it or not.

Unlike me, Vince always seemed to have a plan—or at least he looked like he did. Calm, focused, and methodical, he had a knack for making life look manageable. Maybe he was just as terrified underneath it all, but he wore confidence like a perfectly ironed cassock. Meanwhile, I was nineteen, still loitering around the house, already a spinster by my own dramatic standards. Woe is me! I moved through life like a sloth descending from the canopy—slow, confused, and probably clinging to the wrong branch.

I imagine one day Mom looked at me and thought, "Wait… why are you still here?" That's life in a big family: sometimes you just disappear into the crowd. Your parents forget you're still lurking around, and you forget that you're supposed to be doing something, besides waiting for direction. When you're part of a large tribe, it's easy to become one of many, a background character in your own story. You don't realize you're supposed to be an individual until the others start peeling off and, suddenly, you're standing there, blinking in the spotlight.

Just two teens—Andy and I were remaining at home when mom and dad packed up the bus and moved to Sacramento. Life in California's capital meant endless neighborhoods, all tangled together by a maze of freeways—a blur of impatient, tailgating speed demons. My poor Ford Pinto didn't stand a chance.

So, I sold it, pooled the cash with my junior-mechanic brother, and we bought a '68 Mustang to share. Most people would've called that a disaster waiting to happen, but it worked. We spent every spare dollar and minute under the hood. Test drives felt like rocket launches. On good days, the front end would lift so high you couldn't see the road—but who cared? We were leaving everyone in the dust anyway. On bad days, I'd be pulled over on the shoulder, offering the engine a pep talk.

We split duties: I kept gas in it; he kept it alive. From distributor caps to timing lights, we learned by doing—greasy hands, scraped knuckles, and a lot of trial and error. Breakdown? No big deal. That's what the trunk was for: spare parts, tools, jumper cables, fuel line, and, always, oil. The Mustang leaked like a busted faucet. I could tell how long I'd been parked by the puddle it left behind.

About this time, I also got a job at a deli, and I discovered something wonderful—community college. It cost barely anything, and you did not have to pass an SAT to get in! I drove that Mustang straight up to the admissions office and signed up for my very first classes, Art History, Drafting, and English. I was pleased as punch and off and running a year later than my peers, but at least I

Chapter One: A Young Family

had figured it out, and that is the real lesson in life, how to figure stuff out.

A year later, just as I was settling into my college bliss, my parents dropped the bomb: they were moving again.

"Figure it out," they said, "because we're loading up the bus." I was crushed. I loved college, and for the first time in my life, I felt like I was off to Finishing School, Eleanor Roosevelt-style. But this was a serious problem. My little deli job barely covered gas and gum. There was no way I could afford to live on my own, especially not during a recession when no one was hiring. I had a month to make a plan or be dragged back onto that rolling circus.

"This is it," I told myself. "Now's the time to figure it out, or risk spending the rest of my life in that damn bus."

Right around then, as if on cue, Lorenzo called out of the blue. He had joined the Air Force and, with all the subtlety of a toaster fire, asked, "Hey… ya wanna get married?" So, I said, "Sure!"

Twenty-nine days later, we were married. And I quickly learned that the military's nomadic lifestyle didn't mix with my college dreams. Stability was a myth—either we were stationed in the middle of nowhere with no schools around, or we were packing up for yet another move. To make matters worse, I was now officially classified as a Dependent. That label hit me like a punch. I'd never thought of myself as dependent on anyone, and now the government had stamped it on my identity, right across my forehead. No degree, no career, and now—officially—a nobody.

And so, from Air Force base to Air Force base we went. With every move, I drifted further from college life, but I found solace in the one place that never failed me: the library. Base libraries became my sanctuary. I read like a parched traveler at an oasis—Plato's *Republic*, Cicero, Lucretius' *On the Nature of Things*, and of course, Virgil. One brilliant thought after another, and soon I was scribbling them all down, filling stacks of composition books—a habit carried over from childhood.

But then came a new dilemma: where to keep all these collected writings? A box? A binder? A drawer? The answer arrived one rainy Sunday afternoon, buried in the pages of Thomas Jefferson's letters. He kept a Commonplace Book—a kind of literary scrapbook, where he recorded favorite quotes to remember and reuse. He started the habit while attending Maury's school as a young man.

One of Jefferson's Commonplace Books was filled with passages from John Milton's *Paradise Lost* lines he later drew from when crafting the Declaration of Independence and other founding ideas. Stanford University even held a copy of *Paradise Lost* signed by both Jefferson and James Madison. Jefferson was so devoted to knowledge that he invented a revolving bookstand so he could consult five books at once. I felt like I'd found a kindred spirit—in went my notebooks, into a Commonplace Box.

Why hadn't I paid attention to him in high school? Why don't more teenagers see the brilliance in these early thinkers? It's a mystery. But no matter—I had found him now. I built my own Commonplace Box, filling it with those worn composition books. And in doing so, I found reassurance: I wasn't lost after all. I was simply following a quieter path—a path well-tread by thinkers before me. It's comforting to know that, even when you feel adrift, you're walking in the footsteps of greatness.

Chapter One: A Young Family

The day I discovered Leonardo da Vinci—who proudly called himself "uomo senza lettere" ("a man without letters," meaning no formal education)—I knew I wasn't alone. He also referred to himself as a "discepolo della esperienza"—a "disciple of experience." That was me in a nutshell, especially with all this military travel shaping my schooling.

Born in 1452 near the village of Vinci, Leonardo was illegitimate and considered unworthy of formal schooling. But he didn't just invent or paint masterpieces—he also turned his entire life into a work of art. From jotting down simple lists to unraveling mysteries of architecture, mechanics, philosophy, and even space, everything he touched held hidden beauty. His life was contentious, purposeful, and bursting with passion.

I checked out that book, along with a few others I could carry. A kind stranger saw this juggling act—purse, books, keys—and kindly held the library door for me. "Grazie!" a smile and a nod and out I went to the parking lot. I felt very Italian that day. If Leonardo found a way, so would I.

As Leonardo said, "Learning never exhausts the mind."

Chapter Two

Travel

Even though he died before I was born in 1963, Kennedy's energy, enthusiasm, and vision for America still crackled in the air. The space program was in full throttle, and while the space race between the United States and Russia was just one front in the Cold War, it sparked a surge in education and research. This investment gave rise to "spin-off technologies" like Teflon, Tang, memory foam, freeze-dried food, and even space blankets. For the first time, Americans saw color pictures of Earth from deep space—God's eye view of our tiny blue planet. Everyone benefited, but two things happened especially: pride in being American soared, and countless people found new inspiration to innovate.

Dad needed a name for his masterpiece. Calling it "The Bus" didn't capture the creativity and care he'd poured into it. So, after a long brainstorming session—and inspired by a night at the theater watching *Camelot*, the legendary tale of King Arthur and the Knights of the Round Table—Mom and Dad christened her Camp-a-lot.

The very next morning, Dad emblazoned the name across the side of the bus in big, bold letters: CAMP-A-LOT! At last, she was complete.

Now travel ready, it was time to load her up. Dishes, blankets, sleeping bags, lawn chairs, food, etc. It all went in. There was plenty of room because the Camp-a-lot was a storage engineering marvel.

Chapter Two: Travel

Dad had copied a lot of storage ideas from boats and travel trailers which allowed for every hollow to be filled with something, even extra parts for the engine and repairs. Inside was no exception, a dining room table and eating area by day would turn into a Queen Size bed by night. All eight kids slept in the back; there were two larger sized beds along the side and two more narrow ones on the other side. Not to sugar coat things, there were some design flaws. The worst place to sleep was in the larger size bottom bed. If a kid slept there, near the wall and was startled awake in the middle of the night, they would hit their head on the bed above, smash their face against the wall, turn over and careen into an older sibling! With nowhere to escape, a half asleep and panicked kid would get socked by their older brother or sister and told to be quiet. There were design flaws.

We each had our own "Cubby," is what mom called it, but really it was a hole—we each had our own hole. I figured she thought it would be more palatable and cuter if she called the designated hole to put our clothes in, a Cubby! There was barely enough room for clothes, but mom decided that we also had room for our schoolbooks in there, too, and so in went geometry, English, and composition books. I chose the cubby hole down at the bottom. Since I was the youngest, I did not have much of a choice, and, secondly, it just seemed bigger and would hold more stuff. I guess I did not mind being stepped on occasionally, or maybe my older sister told me I shouldn't mind being stepped on. I forget. Anyway, I had my coveted space for my coveted things and ideas.

The Grand Canyon—our first big adventure—and I, for one, was practically vibrating with excitement. The thought of driving through the desert, meeting real-life Native Americans, and seeing that great big hole in the ground made it impossible to sit still. All ten of us were packed in, plus a couple of bikes, food in every cupboard, and a hefty dose of family optimism. With a creak, a groan, and a puff of exhaust, the mighty Camp-a-lot rumbled out of the backyard, bumped over the driveway, and onto the open road. We were off—eight kids, two parents, zero seatbelts, and one enormous sense of adventure.

It was a lot further than I thought. Dad seemed to drive for days without sleeping; I do not know how he did it. I would go to bed, and he was driving, I would wake up and he was driving. I think he got to escape this way. We would travel about 700 miles and, depending on how much sleep he got, we should get there in a couple of days. But of course, that depended how many breaks dad would need and how many times he would have to break up an argument. "Don't make me stop this bus!" he would shout from behind the wheel, and all would become quiet again. Little Andy, the baby of the crew, found his happy place down in the stairwell by the front door. Clutching a paper plate and wearing a look of intense concentration, he mimicked every turn of the wheel. In his mind, he was co-pilot. In ours, he was adorable—and also blocking the exit.

My favorite spot was the long bench across from Dad, right next to Little Andy's command station. I'd curl up there like a lizard on a warm rock, watching the country glide by in wide panoramic windows, the hum of the tires lulling me into a travel trance.

The one touch of modernity in our time machine on wheels was Dad's beloved eight-track tape player. It was sacred. Hands off.

Chapter Two: Travel

No exceptions. Housed in a handcrafted wooden box, his prized collection included Bill Cosby stand-up, smooth Marvin Gaye, and a whole lot of Neil Diamond. It was a strange musical trifecta, but somehow, it worked—like Dad's driving style: relentless, loud, and oddly comforting.

As we rolled across the desert, Marvin Gaye's smooth voice filled the bus, blending perfectly with the sun-baked stillness outside. At one point, a bird flew up beside us, gliding effortlessly just outside the window. It kept pace with the Camp-a-lot for a good stretch, and I imagined—no, knew—that bird was an angel, sent by God to ride alongside us for a while.

But by the time we hit the city limits, the soundtrack had shifted. Neil Diamond was belting out, "It's a beautiful noise, coming up from the street, it's got a beautiful sound, it's got a beautiful beat." The "beautiful noise" Neil sang about quickly became a chorus of honking horns, screeching brakes, and pedestrians yelling things I wasn't supposed to repeat.

Navigating the Camp-a-lot through a city was not for the faint of heart. It required nerves of steel, lightning-fast reflexes, and—apparently—a wide and creative vocabulary of profanity. I always thought Dad had what it took. In my mind, cussing wasn't swearing, it was just urban navigation language. Still, the irony wasn't lost on me: while Neil Diamond sang about the poetry of city noise, Dad was behind the wheel muttering words that would've earned the rest of us a mouthful of soap.

And then one day, we were there, the Grand Canyon! An ancient thing to new young eyes is an intriguing paradoxical thing. The ancient thing will go on being ancient long after the living have ceased living on this planet, yet it is only the living that can appreciate its magnificence. As dad searched for a place to park, the Grand Canyon in all its majesty rolled past the window, the open sky and the clouds intertwined with the reds and browns in the foreground. I became lost in thought; it was one of my first spiritual experiences. "God was truly the great creator," I thought, and I felt like I was intertwined with my maker. My daydream didn't last long—rarely did. Blaise, allergic to silence, spotted an opportunity. He crept up behind Mom and shoved open the window right next to her head. The wind whooshed in like a freight train. Before anyone could react, he stuck his head out and screamed, "Help me!"

Mom jolted upright. "Oh my God, Andy, stop the bus—we lost one!"

Dad slammed on the brakes as ordered. Blaise howled with laughter, practically falling into the aisle. Mom, clutching her chest like she'd just flatlined, swung around and smacked him.

"Blaise! Oh my God!" she gasped, trying to catch her breath.

Dad gave Blaise the evil eye, the kind that promised future consequences, then shifted gears and we were off again—chaos temporarily restored to order.

When the bus finally came to one of those vista points near the canyon, we all piled out, pushing and shoving through the small bus doors. The great mass of people called my family did not leave much room for the average size adult, but for the smaller younger ones, being small meant survival. A small child can always push themselves to the front by getting smaller still. I popped out of the front doorway and into the hugeness of it all. I felt small, really small, and yet wrapped up in the arms of God. We stayed for it seemed a week. I am not sure we did anything but stare at that great big, huge canyon.

That summer we drove through places that did not really have significance to me as a child, I was only concerned with seeing horses and Native Americans. However, my parents did have a knack for finding the oddest places that a kid would have never thought of, places like Area 51 and the Extraterrestrial Highway. Alongside the highway was a mailbox, just sitting there by itself with a couple of names on it—one was marked, "Alien." Driving the remote areas of Americas wide open spaces, the locals seem to be obsessed with the unusual, but the unusually large; anything to get a driver to stop. The world's largest Pistachio, frying pan, and ball of twine. I did not think about it much as I sat on my bed organizing my box of treasures collected from our stops. This included bubble gum and post cards mostly. That is until my older brother Marc began telling stories of Aliens and how they regularly visit planet earth to suck people's brains out. I told him to stop scaring the younger ones, and he chased me around the bus with one hand shaped like a claw, trying to suck my brains out till mom yelled at him to stop. And then the bus did. Parents know when kids have had enough and need to run—and what better place than the desert. You get a clear view of where they are—nothing but cactus and wide-open spaces, so they can't get lost. And the best thing, they will all come back accounted for. Thirst and fatigue are strong drivers.

One morning, after parking overnight at a campground, we were mid-breakfast when there came a knock at the bus door. I got up to answer it, Marc trailing behind me like a shadow. With a dramatic swoosh, I slid open the two flapped doors. Standing outside was a teenage girl, eyeing our massive rig with amusement.

"Um… hey. You guys the Partridge Family or somethin'?"

Still sore from Marc tormenting me the day before, I seized the moment. With a grin, I turned and shoved him out the door. He stumbled forward, arms flailing, and landed right in her surprised embrace.

"Yeah," I said, deadpan. "And that there's Keith Partridge."

Then I slammed the door shut with perfect comedic timing, leaving them both outside—one stunned, the other embarrassed.

During the summer, Dad would often park the bus at a campground, usually our local Ranch Club—and head off to work during the week, leaving us and Mom to live the campground life. He'd come back on weekends, driving his company truck like some suburban cowboy returning to the homestead. One weekend, he got it into his head that he'd leave us—not just at the Ranch Club—but in Yosemite.

"Andy, you can't be serious," Mom said, eyes wide. "I read in Reader's Digest that a whole family was eaten alive by a bear in Yosemite!"

"Oh, for pity's sake, Pat," Dad replied, brushing it off. "There are rangers everywhere. I can't remember the last time anyone was eaten by a bear up there. You and the kids will be fine."

Spoiler alert: We were not fine. (Okay, we weren't eaten, but still—Yosemite.)

That was the end of that discussion—and a week later, we were camped deep in the valley of Yosemite National Park. The awning was out, a strip of green astroturf rolled across the dirt like a welcome mat, lawn chairs arranged like a suburban living room, and Dad? Gone. Back to work. The air was thick with the smells of woodsmoke, pine needles, and someone's campfire dinner—bacon, maybe, or chili—something hearty and slightly burnt. It mixed with the scent of damp forest floor and the faint whiff of bug spray clinging to our clothes. Mom walked quietly beside me. I remember holding her hand and glancing up at her, wondering—just for a second—what it must feel like to be her: alone with eight kids, parked in bear country, and no escape vehicle. As we passed the restroom and picnic area, she paused to read a sign out loud: "This area known as a bear feeding ground. Pick up and contain all food items." She let out a long sigh but didn't say another word until we got back to the campsite.

That night, she transformed into a nervous little quail, poking her head out from under a blanket and whisper-squeaking orders: "Stay inside. Be quiet. Don't open anything that smells like food."

It didn't help that Marc and Paul kept sneaking up behind her, making low growling noises and pretending to claw at her back.

"Stop it, you two!" she snapped, clutching her *Reader's Digest* like it was bear spray. "I read that bears have been known to rip the doors off cars just to get to an ice chest!"

Marc rolled his eyes, "Mom, we'll be fine."

We made it through the night—no bear attacks, no missing siblings, no claw marks on the Camp-a-lot. By morning, Mom was parked at the window, wrapped tightly in a blanket like a burrito of fear. Only a single steaming mug of coffee poked out, floating eerily as if it had no human attached. The rest of her remained hidden, eyes wide and unblinking, scanning the tree line like a soldier on night watch.

A ranger eventually strolled through the campground, and Mom sprang into action. Robe on, slippers shuffling, she flagged him down with the urgency of someone reporting a crime in progress. I peeked through the window and saw her speaking in hushed tones, her pleading eyes clearly broadcasting one desperate message: bears. After a few minutes, she returned to the table noticeably calmer, poured herself another cup of coffee (her second or tenth, hard to say), and gave us the update.

"Well," she said with a relieved sigh, "the ranger told me there haven't been any bears here in a long, long while. They've just been meaning to take the sign down."

She smiled, practically glowing with caffeine and vindication. "Oh, what a great relief." So that settled it. We could stay. Not necessarily in peace, but at least with the knowledge that the bears had apparently taken an extended vacation—and so could Mom's imagination.

The older boys, Marc and Paul, were thrilled and pulled out their tent. It was known to them as the "Tent of Independence" for obvious reasons, and it meant that they could get away from any dictatorship. They set up their tent not far from the bus but far enough to feel independent. The site they chose, unfortunately, was quickly intruded upon by new campers who had set up their campsite just a stone's throw from the Tent of independence.

"Tommy, you git over here 'fore I clobber you!"

The shout rang out across the campground, delivered by a wild-haired woman who looked like she'd lost a battle with both humidity and parenting. She hurled a crumpled potato chip bag at the back of a redheaded kid's head. He was about five and didn't even flinch—just turned around and shuffled back like it was all part of the daily routine. There was no dad in sight—just her and three kids orbiting her like rowdy moons. She'd tied the family dog to a tree, and it barked from the moment they arrived until well past sunset, like a four-legged car alarm. They operated with the blissful unawareness of people who think the world ends at their tent flaps.

I passed their site on my way to the restroom and stepped right into a fresh pile of their dog's calling card. Disgusted, I plopped down on a log and scraped the mess off my shoe with a stick, muttering a few choice words I'd probably picked up from Dad.

By midday, the chaos had only escalated. So, Vince and I bailed, ducking off to a quiet nature trail and wandering until the sun went down. When we returned, nothing had changed. The noise from that camp still filled the valley—screaming, barking, wrappers rustling like tumbleweeds. It was clear: we weren't going to enjoy ourselves with the Wild Bunch set up fifty feet away. The bears might have been gone—but these people were the real threat to our peace.

Marc, Paul, and Blaise huddled inside the Tent of Independence, plotting revenge. The plan was Blaise's brainchild—naturally—and it would require Marc and Paul to pull it off. Vince, Little Andy, and I wanted in, of course. No good prank was complete without a supporting cast. Marc slung his arms around the three of us and whispered like a general before battle: "Okay, when I say go, you scream and run like maniacs out of the tent. Got it?"

"Yep," we chorused, dead serious.

We waited for nightfall like commandos. Watched. Waited. Watched some more. My eyelids grew heavy, hope was fading, and then—finally—the last lantern in the noisy camp flicked off. Showtime. Marc and Paul struck first, banging pots and pans like deranged pioneers, flinging random gear into the air.

"Now!" Marc hissed.

We launched into action—Vince, Little Andy, and I burst from the tent like it was on fire, howling like wolves with megaphones. We gave it everything we had. Then Blaise made his entrance.

Drenched in ketchup and wielding a butcher knife, he sprinted into the enemy camp just as their tent zipper buzzed open. The second a head popped out, Blaise pointed, eyes wide and ketchup-dripping, and screamed at the top of his lungs:

"Beeeaaaar!"

That was all they needed. They didn't even look. They just tore down their tent, threw it in the back of their camper van, started their engine, and took off. We watched and waited till their camper was out of sight and then fell to the ground in hysterics. For a good hour, we kept re-living the impeccable acting from us younger ones, to the brilliance of the plan and, of course, Blaise's' creative use of ketchup and running with a Butcher Knife, which we were too young to know the stupidity of that. Still, it was brilliantly executed, and we relished it and only calmed down when we looked up at the bus, there peering through parted curtains was the most horrified look on mom's face I had ever seen.

♣

Chapter Two: Travel

When you're newly married, it feels like you're building your own personal Camelot—minus the castles and draw bridges, but definitely with the same starry-eyed ambition. You imagine this shining realm where love rules, loyalty never wavers, and the dishwasher loads itself. You and your spouse are noble knights, galloping off on a quest for the good life, armed with matching luggage and a joint checking account.

But real life, like the tale of Camelot, has a way of swerving off-script. Somewhere between "I do" and "what the hell just happened?" betrayal creeps in sometimes loud, sometimes quiet—and hearts break not with a bang, but with the slow ache of unmet expectations. That's how it was with Lorenzo and I; full of hope, full of love, and full of delusions that our marriage would somehow dodge the curse of history.

Our fairytale began with a descent, literally. As the plane broke through the clouds, I pressed my nose to the window like a kid spotting Disneyland. Crete unfurled below us: a jagged, green jewel rising from the Aegean Sea. Iraklion, the capital, looked like something out of a travel brochure for gods—sun-washed hills, turquoise coastlines, and the kind of light that made everything look blessed.

Lorenzo beamed. "Everyone says I hit the jackpot getting stationed here. Beats getting sent to B.F. Egypt."

"What's B.F. Egypt?" I asked, wide-eyed. He smirked and leaned in. "Bum F#@$ Egypt."

My polite Catholic ears turned crimson. I scribbled a mental note: *must learn new acronyms.*

Before we left the States, I tried to do my homework. I learned that Crete was once the heart of the Minoan civilization—a society so advanced, they had plumbing, fashion sense, and were not too keen on war in spite of the fact that the island had been conquered by just about everyone: Mycenaeans, Romans, Venetians, and Turks. And apparently, the locals hadn't forgotten that last one. I jotted down one piece of survival wisdom in my travel journal: *"Do not, under any circumstance, mention the Turks to the Cretans."*

Crete was a thriving culture from the 27th century before Christ to the 15th century B.C. British archeologist, Arthur Evans, referred to it as "the first link in the European chain." During the Middle Paleolithic age, ancient people settled there as early as 128,000 B. C. 5000 years B. C. they developed agriculture, and that put them at the beginning of civilization.

The plane began its decent about the time my last book hit the floor and my eyes began to close again. It was late in the evening, just before sunset. Our long journey from California to the island of Crete finally came to an end—after multiple flight changes, stiff legs, questionable airplane meals, and a growing suspicion that we might never see our luggage again. As we stepped off the plane and descended the stairs, the smell of the salty sea air was a refreshing change from the inside of the airplane cabin. Walking into the terminal, we were engulfed by a soundscape both unfamiliar and mesmerizing. Voices bartering, prices called out with gusto, laughter rising and falling in rhythm with the lyrical cadence of Greek. The air inside the terminal was thick with the scent of roasted meat, strong coffee, and something vaguely sweet, maybe honey or sun-warmed pastry. Vendors showed no sign of slowing down despite the late hour, circling us like cheerful, persistent bees, their hands gesturing, their smiles wide, eager to part us from our American dollars. Neon lights buzzed overhead, casting a warm, flickering glow on the tiled floor worn smooth by thousands of footsteps. Then, pushing his way through the crowd, came our Sponsor—a stocky, good-natured sergeant in his mid-thirties. He greeted us with a firm handshake and a warm grin, then wasted no time hustling us toward a waiting cab. The whole transaction happened so fast, I half-expected someone to hand me a fake passport and whisper, "You were never here."

As the cab sped along the coastal highway, the Mediterranean shimmered beside us, catching the last golden light of day. I caught glimpses of fishermen down on the docks, wrapping up for the night—slapping what I first thought were wet towels against the rocks. A second glance revealed they were squid. Being tenderized. With rocks. The drive stretched on, the moon now high, casting a thick golden ribbon across the dark water. It was breathtaking. The place, the smells, the people—it was all so new, so vivid, so alive that I felt a kind of happy dizziness settle over me. And before I could stop it, a little giggle of delight slipped out of my mouth.

As the cab turned inland, the landscape shifted into something resembling high desert—low, scrubby shrubs, a scattering of trees, and acres upon acres of vineyards. Then, just as night fully settled in, there appeared to be hundreds of small white mounds scattered across the hills, curiously glowing faintly in the moonlight. Whatever they were, I'd have to wait until morning to find out.

Checking into the Hotel Mykonos that night felt just as surreal. The architecture was pure postcard Greece—whitewashed walls, cobalt trim, marble underfoot—but I was too tired to admire it properly. We found our room, dropped our bags, and collapsed face-first onto the bed without another word.

Morning peeled back the night like a curtain, and when I stepped onto the balcony, I froze. The Mediterranean shimmered below, a sweep of liquid sapphire dotted with lazy white boats swaying in the harbor. Sunlight danced on the marble rail. For a moment, I thought we'd been assigned the wrong room, this wasn't a hotel; it was a palace. I half-expected a bellhop to salute and ask if General and Mrs. Somebody needed anything else. But no—just an airman and his wide-eyed wife, somehow mistaken for royalty.

Still not convinced, I located the front door—tucked neatly behind a pair of velvet drapes—and made my way down the marble staircase to the lobby. The clerk greeted me with a knowing smile, as if she'd seen this exact scene play out before. I leaned in and asked her to double-check our reservation, certain we'd wandered into the officer's quarters by mistake. She tapped a few keys, nodded cheerfully, and confirmed: *Yes, ma'am, this is your room.*

That's when it dawned on me—I'd been thinking like a history buff, not a budget-conscious traveler. I'd read all about the drachma—one of the world's earliest coins, once worth a handful of arrows, depending on the century—but hadn't given the modern exchange rate a second glance. Two drachmas to the dollar. Ah. That would explain the grand staircase, the ocean view, and why, for one brief, marble-clad moment, I felt like I'd married into royalty.

Elegant signs throughout the hotel boasted: *Free Continental Breakfast!* The phrase had a certain ring—something refined, indulgent. Visions of silver trays, croissants stacked like golden pil-

Chapter Two: Travel

lows, maybe a soft-boiled egg in a delicate porcelain cup, danced in the mind.

A seat was taken. A cloth napkin unfolded with great expectation. Moments later, a tiny cup of jet-black coffee arrived—no cream, no sugar—followed by a single, modest roll. No butter in sight. No eggs sizzling in the distance. No sausage making its triumphant entrance.

Polite patience gave way to quiet confusion. The waiter returned, not with more food, but with a nod.

Apparently… that was it.

Continental breakfast: not so much a meal as a vague suggestion served with a side of disappointment.

Later that morning, it was time for Lorenzo to get "in-processed"—military speak for checking in with the boss. Our cheerful sergeant reappeared, now driving his own car, and off we went toward the base, just a couple of miles away. No sooner had the journey begun than the mystery of the white mounds spotted earlier was solved: sheep and goats. Thousands of them. Crete, it turns out, is home to over a million.

The car came to a sudden stop. An ocean of wool and hooves spilled across the highway, moving with the calm authority of creatures that clearly had the right of way. Not a single driver seemed the least bit perturbed; this was simply how mornings went on the island. The herd pressed close, brushing against the car in waves, making the vehicle sway gently, as if breathing.

Laughter bubbled up—what a wonderful, bizarre place. Lorenzo, less enchanted, gripped the door handle and muttered, "What is up with all these stupid sheep?"

The base was small and utilitarian—boxy gray buildings lined up like a set of oversized filing cabinets. A base exchange, a sports field, a modest medical clinic—each structure labeled with a letter and number, the military's idea of architectural flair. Opportunities for a Dependent were limited: no college, no shops, no café to linger in with a book and a pastry. But there was a library. A quiet little lifeboat of knowledge.

So, the next three years were divided simply: Lorenzo went to work, and the library became home.

One thing about being young and in the military: nearly everyone's newly married, wildly hormonal, and either pregnant or headed there at full speed. Sex wasn't just recreational—it felt like the base's unofficial sport. Especially when married to a Latin lover. Passion wasn't optional; it was the daily special.

Naturally, this new phase of life sparked a deep curiosity about women's health. Books were devoured, articles dog-eared, medical pamphlets hoarded. Eventually, armed with far too much information and a queasy sense of obligation, an appointment was made for the dreaded "female checkup."

Nothing could have prepared me.

The infamous Pap smear—marketed as a quick screen for cervical cancer—was both physically uncomfortable and mentally... perplexing. Of all the body parts, why so much scrutiny on *that* one? There are *hundreds* of cancers. Why such a laser focus on the Hoo-ha? With diabetes at epidemic levels, wouldn't checking insulin be more urgent? And what about colon cancer, or skin cancer, or anything else less...intimate?

It all started to feel less like medicine and more like a suspiciously vagina-centric conspiracy. I made a quiet vow then and there: *avoid gynecologists at all costs*. That is, of course, until two pink lines changed everything.

Lorenzo's parents were ecstatic—new titles bestowed: *Grandparents!* Lorenzo himself was downright euphoric. On the way to the Air Force Commissary, he strutted like a peacock, chest puffed, declaring to anyone within a five-foot radius, "*I did that!*"—as if he'd single-handedly discovered pregnancy and generously shared it with the world.

Meanwhile, I was cautiously silent. Because women know—without needing to be told—that carrying another human being isn't just about swollen ankles and prenatal vitamins. It's weight in every sense of the word: emotional, spiritual, unyielding. From that moment on, life shifts. It's no longer yours alone. And it never will be again.

Determined to save every penny for the baby, the rule was clear: no unnecessary spending. February arrived, bringing my birthday wrapped in quiet restraint. When he walked through the door with empty hands, the floodgates opened—tears slipping down uninvited.

"I thought you said not to get you anything," he said, genuinely baffled.

"That's not *what* I meant," came the sniffled confession, words tangled in tears.

Lesson one: decoding the subtle language of pregnant wives is a must—missteps come with emotional consequences.

But then, like a man on a mission, he reappeared an hour later, brandishing a crock pot adorned with a bright bow. The absurdity of a slow cooker as a birthday gift hit the funny bone hard—tears turned to laughter, filling the room with a perfect mix of love and resignation.

Pregnancy didn't slow the adventure. Willing to go anywhere, the Vespa became the chariot of choice—an Italian scooter named for the wasp, buzzing through Crete's winding roads. Every month or so, downtown Iraklion called. Vespas were rented, engines hummed, and the island unfolded like a secret map waiting to be explored.

Helmetless, wind in the face, belly rounding with each mile, freedom felt absolute. No rules, no warnings from agency or parents—ignorance was bliss on two wheels.

One afternoon, as the scooter zipped past a street-side food stand, a scent slammed into the senses—smoky, savory pork, turning slowly on a giant spit under the golden sun. Momentum faltered. The nose led straight to a pita stand, eyes locked on the meat's slow dance.

Drool threatened escape. Glancing up, the heavyset Greek cook in his stained white apron met the gaze.

"What is that smell?" came the inevitable question.

He laughed. "Why, it's Peeta!"

"Whatever it is," came the words between licks of drool wiped from a very pregnant chin, "one, please."

A few drachma—about fifty cents—exchanged hands, and a grin spread across the cook's face. "Me ola?" he asked, which later

Chapter Two: Travel

turned out to mean "with everything." No clue what "everything" entailed, but a confident nod sealed the deal.

Minutes later, a masterpiece appeared: a warm pita wrapped in red-and-white checked paper, bursting with creamy tzatziki—yogurt, dill, cucumber, lemon, purple onion, and tomatoes—all snuggling a pile of perfectly seasoned pork.

Settling at a small round table, the first bite brought everything to a halt. A burst of unexpected flavor—bold, fresh, and utterly unlike anything from childhood's cautious palate. Onions weren't to be feared, yogurt could be delicious, and dill was suddenly a revelation.

That day, a quiet lesson unfolded: childhood often masks a world waiting to be discovered. Age, experience, and a touch of humility were the keys to fully experiencing the new. Sometimes, it's as small as a pita.

That was it—the taste of Greece had been found. A culinary revelation that quickly became the prime culprit behind a twenty-pound pregnancy weight gain. In America, they're called gyros—an almost-accurate name, but only part of the story.

Gyro means "turn" or "rotation," a nod to the vertical spit stacked high with thin slices of pork, slowly spinning before glowing electric bars in countless pita shops across Crete. As the meat turns, fat melts and drips, sizzling as it falls. The cone of pork crisps beautifully at the edges while remaining juicy and tender inside.

But to simply call it a Gyro ignores so much more! The pita bread is brushed with olive oil and grilled until warm and just a touch crispy, ready to cradle the magic within, freshly sliced onion,

Tzatziki sauce and tomatoes. The whole glorious, salty, greasy masterpiece is wrapped tight—often with a generous handful of French fries (or "chips," as they're known across Europe), fresh and piping hot from the fryer. Add more if you're pregnant.

Some months later, after waddling my way through pregnancy cravings and unsolicited belly rubs from strangers, our very first child arrived, a little boy. He came into the world red-faced and howling, as if personally offended by the bright lights of the delivery room.

Lorenzo and I had wrestled for weeks with the impossible task of naming him. Every suggestion turned into a negotiation. We vetoed trendy names, names of exes, names of annoying coworkers, and anything that sounded like a sneeze. Eventually, we landed on "Anthony." It was classic. Strong. Saintly. It could be tender and lyrical—*An-tho-ny*—or New York tough—*Tony*. Plus, the name came with an all-star roster: St. Anthony, patron of lost things (perfect for new parents), Mark Antony (close enough), Anthony Hopkins (distinguished), and, of course, Tony Danza (underrated national treasure).

We'd prepared for everything—crib assembled, onesies folded, car seat installed with the precision of a NASA engineer. But nothing could have prepared me for what actually happened: I fell head-over-heels, all-in, no-turning-back in love with him. Not "oh-he's-cute" love. I mean cracked-open, soul-altering, hand-holding-an-angel kind of love.

He smelled like powdered sugar and possibility. I could barely stop staring at him. Every twitch of his mouth felt like a message from Heaven. He was tiny, perfect, and mine. And in those first

Chapter Two: Travel

days, when I looked into his sleepy, searching eyes, one word kept coming to mind: **God**. That's it. Just God. As if God had looked at Lorenzo and me, smiled, and said, *Here you go—try not to mess this one up.*

Sure, science can explain maternal bonding with a cocktail of hormones and evolutionary instincts. But that's just the instruction manual. The real miracle is what happens in your heart. You're not just caring for someone—you're changing. It's like your soul rearranges itself overnight. Suddenly, someone else's needs override your own, and not out of duty, but joy. That's the kicker.

No book, birth class, or baby video could've prepared me for it. It was like I'd been walking around with blinders my whole life. And now, for the first time, I could see. Or as the song goes—*Amazing Grace* and all—"I once was blind, but now I see."

And so, my days became a marathon paced to the cries of a newborn. The only surefire way to keep him from wailing? Walk. Not rock, not bounce, not sing—walk. I became a stroller-bound nomad, a connoisseur of sidewalks, memorizing every crack, bump, and jolt-worthy stretch within a five-mile radius. The rougher the ride, the deeper he slept. I had a theory that if I ever hit a pothole just right, he might nap until college.

One afternoon, during one of our endless loops around base housing, I found myself slowing in front of the library. Just outside the entrance stood a sun-bleached bulletin board, the word *WANTED* scrawled across the top like an old Western poster. I stepped closer, stroller brakes squeaking, half expecting to see a bounty notice for a rogue toddler.

Most of the cards were the usual: "Reliable babysitter needed," "Cafeteria help wanted," "Buy one Tupperware, get one free." But one index card, crooked and barely clinging to the cork, caught my eye: <u>Volunteer at the Dental Clinic. Red Cross. No pay.</u>

It didn't pay. But it did something else—it sparked. Maybe it was the idea of speaking to adults again. Maybe it was the promise of learning something new that didn't involve diaper brands. Either way, I spun the stroller around like I was charging into battle and marched straight to the Red Cross office.

Inside, I found a lone woman hunched over a desk, peeling off ancient contact paper with the grim determination of someone losing a fight to both time and glue. She looked up, startled, and then broke into a smile so wide, you'd think she'd been waiting all year for someone to walk through that door.

By week's end, a stiff blue volunteer smock hung on a borrowed hook, and mornings started with a jolt—three times a week, no pay, all purpose. Not everyone shared the enthusiasm. Lorenzo, for one, sulked like unpaid labor was a personal betrayal.

The base dental clinic ran on caffeine and chaos. Patients shuffled through like reruns. Mrs. Beaterman was on constant rotation. Chronic TMJ—translation: her jaw hurt, and nobody could fix it. She'd seen every dentist, every specialist, even the guy who usually fixed aircraft hydraulics. Still hurting.

Military care on an island had a rhythm: no competition, no consequences. One clinic, one option. Burnout behind the desk, frustration in the waiting room. Everyone was tired.

A familiar stomp sounded outside—tight shoulders, clenched fists, head angled forward like a battering ram. Mrs. Beaterman.

Chapter Two: Travel

A hand yanked on my smock from down behind the desk. Dentist's Jim and Dave were already there, crouched like fugitives behind enemy lines.

"Flip the open sign to closed, Becca. Now," Dave hissed, nodding toward the front.

She hadn't even reached the window yet, but the air already felt heavier. And next to her? Mr. Beaterman, the human embodiment of a dental malpractice lawsuit, that is if the military would allow such a thing!

Moving into a low crawl, the CLOSED sign slid into place. One beat. Two. She reached the glass, read the sign, spun on her heel, and stormed off.

Silence.

Then Dave, whispering like a man newly baptized: "God bless office supplies."

He slumped back against the filing cabinet. "I got her a consult in Germany next week. Already loaded her up with enough Vicodin to down an elephant. I don't know what else to do!"

The sign got a laugh, sure—but something twisted in the gut. That little voice, the moral compass, piped up again. It always did.

In those early years, doing the right thing often clashed with doing the only thing. That compass? Reliable. Also annoying. And it would complicate a lot more than just a Tuesday morning with the Beatermans.

In the military, drinking isn't just a pastime; it's practically a hobby. And Lorenzo? A committed enthusiast. Every weekend, he disappeared into a booze-soaked haze, usually dragging his buddy Larry along for the ride.

One night, he finally stumbled home around two, reeking of beer and bravado, and collapsed onto the bed like a downed oak. Within minutes, the snoring began—deep, uneven blasts like a freight train with engine trouble.

Just as sleep started to creep in, a knock shattered the quiet. Not a gentle tap, but a relentless pounding that rattled the doorframe. The clock glowed at 2:15 a.m.

Larry.

"Are you going to get that?" The whisper barely made it past clenched teeth.

Lorenzo groaned, peeled himself off the mattress, and shuffled down the hallway, trying not to wake the baby. The front door creaked open.

There stood Larry, swaying, shirt half-buttoned, eyes glassy. He wore the smirk of a man with no regrets and no boundaries. "Hey there, Lorenzo," he slurred, as if it were cocktail hour and not the middle of the night.

"Hey, I need a push," Larry called out.

"No, Larry. Walk home."

Lorenzo slammed the door and flopped back into bed.

"That wasn't very Christian of you," I whispered, glaring into the dark. "Think of all the people who've helped you. Where would you be if no one ever lent a hand? If your friend needs help starting his car, you should go help."

A groan rose from the pillow beside me. "He's not stranded on the Autobahn—he lives three doors down. He can get his car tomorrow."

Chapter Two: Travel

Due to the loss of innocence from my childhood, I did not see things as funny as they might have been as a kid, I began to lose my patience, "That's not the point," I said, channeling every Sunday school teacher I'd ever had. "If someone needs help, you help."

With the enthusiasm of a martyr heading to the lions, Lorenzo threw off the blanket, muttered something about sainthood, and shuffled down the hall. The door creaked open.

"Larry?"

Nothing.

He stepped outside, scanned the yard. "Larry?"

From the shadows came the slurred response: "Over here, man! I'm on your kid's swing. I need a push."

This, I decided, was the final straw in the Lorenzo-and-Larry Late Night Circus. If I wanted to save my husband from pickling his liver with that lovable idiot, I needed a better strategy than moral guilt. I needed distance. A continental divide.

So, I proposed a two-week trip through Europe. Just the two of us. My grandmotherly friend who ran a home daycare offered to watch our son, and with that, the plan was set.

We booked flights through the military's Space-A system, a travel "deal" best described as: *Bring your sense of adventure and a sturdy spine.* For under a hundred bucks, we scored seats—well, a spot—on a cargo plane. Forget rows or aisles. There were no seats, just a floor and a cargo net strung along the side like a makeshift hammock from a pirate ship.

Lunch came in a paper sack hurled into your lap with military precision, and the preflight safety briefing was basically: "Strap in, shut up, and hang on."

But it was cheap. And if you were young, broke, and starved for a thrill, it felt like an upgrade from economy class. Somehow, bouncing around in a flying warehouse with no windows counted as "romantic European adventure" when you were in your twenties and trying to outrun your husband's drinking buddy.

Our youthful adventure kicked off in Naples, then swept through Rome, with a mandatory pilgrimage to the Vatican. Everywhere the eye landed—architecture soaring skyward, stained glass windows casting kaleidoscopic light, intricate mosaics sparkling underfoot, towering columns, and the legendary Colosseum—each marvel begged for a neck-craning stare that left muscles aching from the constant whip of my head.

But all the grandeur in the world felt like background noise without someone to breathe life into it. After a day-long hunt for a decent tour guide, we hit the jackpot: Emilia. Tall and slender, with dark hair pulled back tight, she carried an energy that crackled like lightning on a stormy night. Middle-aged and fiery, Emilia wasn't just recounting facts—she was delivering raw, unfiltered history with the heart of a kindergarten teacher and the brain of a professor.

Her passion was contagious. As she rattled off tales of statues, bridges, ancient roads, and monumental buildings, the whole bus lit up. Smiles spread like wildfire. Emilia's knowledge wasn't just impressive—it made the past pulse with life, turning stone and marble into stories.

Next stop: the Pantheon. Stepping into the vast, echoing chamber, all eyes were drawn upward to the oculus—an open eye at the dome's apex—framing a perfect circle of sky. Originally built in 27

Chapter Two: Travel

BC by Marcus Agrippa and later rebuilt by Emperor Hadrian between 118 and 128 AD as a tribute to the Pagan gods, the Pantheon still stood rock-solid, a testament to ancient engineering and stubborn faith.

By 313, Constantine's Edict of Milan had legalized Christian worship, and by the seventh century, this pagan temple had been repurposed as a Roman Catholic church. Emilia pointed out the fascinating coexistence inside—the lingering Pagan frescoes, empty shelves once meant for idols, and relics side-by-side with Christian icons, a visual collision of civilizations and beliefs.

As the tour wrapped, a hunger for more history gnawed at me. Spotting another group, I tried to sneak in—no payment, all charm. The ruse lasted approximately thirty seconds before I was spotted and politely but firmly escorted out.

Getting away with things had never been a strong suit, and a grudging admiration grew in me for those with the skill to pull it off—not out of rebellion, but sheer audacity and hutzpah. A mental note was made, *practice my hutzpah.*

England was the final leg of our journey: Madame Tussauds, Big Ben's chimes, Buckingham Palace's grandeur, and the storied halls of Cambridge. But before calling it done, there was one more must-see—a castle. Warwick Castle, perched majestically on a bend of the Avon River, was the obvious choice.

Tickets in hand, we stepped inside the sprawling fortress. Our guide, George, was a small, sprightly man with a thick British accent and a waistcoat so sharp it could have cut the tension in the room. He looked like he'd just stepped out of a historical reenactment—or a very well-dressed time capsule.

"Built by William the Conqueror," George began, "this fortress served as a military stronghold until the early 17th century when Sir Fulke Greville decided it was time for an upgrade—turning it into a country house. A rather fancy one, mind you."

George's enthusiasm was infectious as he rattled off tales of power plays and prisoner shuffles. "The castle was taken in 1153 by Henry of Anjou, who later became Henry II. Over the centuries, it played host to prisoners from the Battle of Poitiers and, in a rather dramatic twist, Richard Neville—known as 'Warwick the Kingmaker'—used it to lock up King Edward IV himself."

I couldn't help but picture the royal prisoner pacing those ancient halls, probably wondering why he'd agreed to a castle stay that was anything but a vacation.

As George spun history with theatrical flair, the castle's stones seemed less like cold rock and more like the original gossip column—full of intrigue, backstabbing, and enough drama to rival any soap opera.

Standing in that ancient castle, surrounded by stories of kings, queens, and valiant knights, the mind naturally drifts back to a different kind of kingdom—Camp-a-lot, a chaotic Italian Catholic family bus from not so long ago.

As a child, those images were vivid and thrilling—full of adventure and the promise of loyalty and honor. But revisiting Camelot as an adult reveals a far more complicated tale. Guinevere's affair with Lancelot is one of history's most infamous betrayals, the spark that set King Arthur's kingdom crumbling.

The mature mind asks why they "did it," knowing what was at stake. The simplest answer? Because it's complicated. The deeper truth involves the crushing pressure to be perfect, the lure of forbidden love, and sometimes, just plain thoughtlessness.

Arthur loved both Guinevere, his wife, and Lancelot, his closest friend—each in his own way, deeply and differently. He also loved the ideal he had forged: the Knights of the Round Table, a code of trust so sacred that once broken, it could never be fully restored—only limp along as a fading shadow of what it once was.

Left heartbroken, Arthur mourned not only his marriage and friendship but his fractured kingdom. Doubt crept in—could a realm born of such imperfection survive in a world so prone to falling?

That question lingered with me then—and would return again, weaving through my thoughts in the years to come.

The suits of armor lining the dining room walls immediately drew the eye—not just for their intricate craftsmanship, but for their surprisingly small size. Clearly made for men much shorter and slimmer than my six-foot-two Lorenzo, with his broad shoulders and equally broad appetite. Historians chalk it up to centuries of chronic malnutrition, failed crops, and meager diets.

But standing in those cavernous medieval kitchens, it was hard to picture such scarcity. The heavy scent of smoke and burning wood hung thick in the air, punctuated by the rhythmic clatter of pots and pans and the occasional bark of a cook's orders. Gigantic hearths roared with flame, their heat pressing against the skin like a living thing.

Even the simplest loaf of bread demanded an army of servants, their footsteps echoing in narrow, dark corridors. These workers lived packed tight in shared quarters, where beds barely allowed a full stretch, and privacy was a forgotten luxury. The walls themselves whispered the unvarnished truth: here, physical space—and personal comfort—were measured by social rank, doling out privilege in inches and elbow room.

Seeing those small suits of armor early in the tour framed everything that followed—not as relics made for children, but the actual size of grown men from centuries past. It gave the castle an eerie intimacy, and maybe a hint of sympathy for Lorenzo's struggle to fit into his own armor some days.

The tour ended in the dungeon. Hanging above us was a tiny metal cage, swaying slightly like a grim little chandelier. Inside, rattled human bones—silent witnesses to a time when prison conditions made today's worst traffic jams look like luxury.

Those bones had once belonged to someone's child.

I stared upward, stunned. Who were they? What had happened? And who, if anyone, had shed a tear?

In that moment, the castle walls faded away. No longer just a tourist admiring old stones, I was a mother.

Mothers don't see history in bones; they see a baby—someone's lost little one.

Our vacation was over. Time to head home. And though the trip had been unforgettable, the biggest adventure was waiting—raising my son. The ache of missing him settled deep, like a slow, persistent tide pulling at the shore—quiet, relentless, and impossible to ignore.

Chapter Three

Innovation

Outside, the leaves had turned a striking palette of orange, yellow, and pale green. They quivered in the wind, swayed like dancers, then gently broke free from their branches. Fall had arrived, and with it, the new school year.

That Saturday morning, we were all piled on the sofa watching cartoons—dreading Monday like a line of little soldiers awaiting execution. Then the front door swung open, and in he came. Dad, with his red hair tousled across his forehead and the biggest grin on his face. Tucked under one arm, wrapped snug in his jacket, was her.

"Look, kids—a puppy."

Vincent was off the couch like a shot, skidding to his knees on the floor. "Put her down here, Daddy! Put her down here!" he begged. Dad lowered the bundle gently, and in a blink she was surrounded by a tangle of reaching hands and gasps of joy.

"Easy now," Dad said. "Don't scare her."

She was a female German Shepherd with soft brown eyes and a black face. Little tan eyebrows arched over her eyes, giving her a sweet, expressive look—almost like she was listening to every word we said. Vince squealed, "What are we going to name her?!"

Just then, Mom walked in and answered without hesitation: "Heidi. She's German, so she should have a German name." Mom was the Namer of things. She'd christened the Camp-a-lot. She named all of us after saints. She believed names mattered—not just here, but eternally. "When you die," she once said, "God will call you by name. So, it better be a good one."

Dad looked down at Heidi with unmistakable pride, his new acquisition. "Look at her paws," he said. "She's going to be a big dog." I looked down at my own feet and quietly wondered if that was true for me, too.

Marc, ever the practical one said, "Dad, she looks purebred, where did she come from." Dad explained that Heidi was indeed papered and cost $400.00, normally, but... he had done a lot of work for this fellow fixing his cars, etc. and they guy had come into hard times and was not able to pay. He had a pair of German Shepherds; the female was expecting a litter of pups, so he said that dad could have the pick in exchange for the work he had done. As I listened it did not escape me that it really was somethin' when someone could do something with their hands of value, and it produced money, or something you wanted or needed in exchange.

Heidi took up the rest of the weekend. For the younger kids, she was never far away, a little blanket cave was created, filled with dishes of dog food, water, and small children. As evening approached, Mom would plead, "Kids, come and eat." Vincent, like a gopher emerging from its burrow, reluctantly obeyed.

As Heidi grew, she immediately took her place in the family. She knew she was not a kid like the rest of us. She belonged to dad, and we were his pups. She accepted her role as sometimes playmate and sometimes protector. Going to the lake meant a day of work for this loyal dog, as all eight children would run screaming towards the water. She was convinced one of us would drown and

Chapter Three: Innovation

her self-appointed job was lifeguard for the duration of the visit. Chaos reigned, discarded blankets, plastic buckets and pairs of flip flops flying into the air, hitting the ground in a giant multicolored mound. As the herd descended into the lake, splashing water, high into the air, she stayed on the shore, wide-eyed patiently pacing-watching, and looking for a drowning victim to drag out.

Marc and Paul were deep in battle—armed with long, stringy water moss pulled from the lake's edge. The lime-green goo made for excellent ammunition: if launched just right, it would splatter across your opponent's face and stick. Pausing to peel it off gave the attacker prime opportunity to strike again.

Before long, both of them looked like swamp monsters—creatures straight out of the Black Lagoon. Their messy warfare drove the younger ones to scatter in retreat, each of us finding a new corner of the lake to claim as a safe zone.

Heidi, in her usual dignified way, stayed far from the fray. But suddenly, her ears perked up and her gaze locked onto something across the shore. There, lying facedown in the shallow water, was Little Andy—snorkel strapped on, peering at pollywogs. Heidi didn't wait. She dove in with a splash, swam across with purpose, and grabbed the waistband of his oversized swim trunks in her teeth. With great effort, she tugged him toward dry land. Unfortunately, her rescue technique had one side effect: as she pulled, Andy's baggy trunks began to slip. By the time she dragged him out of the water, she had not only saved his life (in her mind), but also managed to expose his five-year-old bare butt to the entire lakefront.

"Heaay," he bellowed, as he spit the snorkel out of his mouth, madly swiping at her as he yanked his trunks up. She ran back to the shore, proud and sure that she had "rescued him."

Off on his own in a shady little cove, Vincent stood ankle-deep in hopping frogs, utterly enchanted. His face beamed, and both fists were clenched tight—his idea of treasure. Blaise, unable to stand not knowing, marched over and pried one of Vincent's fists open. Frogs! A squirming pile of them—so many that their tiny legs were bent in all the wrong directions.

"Mommm! Vincent's squishing frogs!"

When the bus pulled into the Napa Valley Ranch Club, it got a lot of stares. As a kid, you think it's cool; as a teenager, you are mortified; as an adult and creator, you could care less what people thought. Dad drove the Camp-a-lot straight to its designated camping site. An annual membership came with a lot of perks, swimming pool, café, game room, creek, walking and bike paths, ceramics shops, tennis courts, and the most beloved thing in my world, horse stables. If I was lucky, my parents would fork over their precious hard-earned dollars for me to have a ride, but not all the time. On days I was not running with my pack of brothers and sisters, I could be found across the stables in the park, sitting at the top of a slide, staring at and smelling these beautiful creatures. I could see everything from this vantage point, the horses being brushed, worked in the round pen and arena. I was memorized by their beauty and strength as they danced on those spindly legs kicking up the dust. It was enough to watch them because at a young age I realized that wanting and having are two different things.

Chapter Three: Innovation

Innovation was the family's unspoken creed—making do with what you had wasn't just necessity, it was art. And on days when I wasn't at the lake or mesmerized by horses, constructing a personal fort became my grandest ambition. After all, what kid doesn't dream of a space all their own? Hauling items from base camp to my "property" gave me the thrilling illusion of independence. I alone decided what counted as essential: a swimsuit, a towel, some old sheets, and a jar of marshmallow cream.

My fortress was a humble Manzanita bush, transformed with a single sheet draped over a sturdy branch and secured with rocks. Ingenious shelves—flat sticks balanced between larger stones—held my precious supplies: Band-Aids, washcloths, a bottle of water, and a tin of cherry-flavored children's aspirin. And no proper hideaway was complete without a loyal companion—so naturally, I brought the dog.

"Heidi!" Come here girl." I enticed her with the marshmallow cream which did not appeal to her in the least, as she walked on by dragging the sheet off the branch with her wagging tail.

Every now and then, Vincent or Little Andy would wander over for a visit, but never Blaise. Blaise didn't believe in tea parties or casual guests—forts, to him, meant battle. His encampments were legendary: fortified strongholds of mystery and menace. Where he found his building materials, I'll never know. One fort had an old box spring mattress for a gate, walls built from rocks shaped like adobe bricks, and narrow windows just wide enough to poke a cannon barrel through.

And his outfit? Equally formidable. He wore a belt fashioned from rope and twine, looped with assorted knives and hand-crafted weapons. A slingshot hung at the ready, and slung over his shoulder was his pièce de résistance—a burlap sack full of dried horse manure, his version of ammunition.

It was late in the afternoon when Blaise finally resurfaced, launching his assault on my peaceful tea party with a single, strategic move: he whistled for the dog. Heidi, my loyal companion—my fort-mate, my sentinel—bolted from her nap and ran straight to him. Traitor.

"Light of Albion, guide my hand," he cried and then came the bombardment. A storm of dried horse manure rained down on my poor Manzanita sheet, thudding like enemy fire. Before I could even grab my marshmallow cream provisions, Blaise was in my space, standing just outside the last trembling flap of my once-proud fort.

He shouted, "Okay, now pretend you're Guinevere—come out so the soldiers can arrest you!"

I barked at Blaise, "I most certainly will not be part of your twisted imagination." I ran for it and dove behind some boulders, and as luck would have it, like manna from heaven - I found a pile of not dried manure, but fresh! I waited until he was close and then threw it as hard as I could. I would have loved it if it hit his face, but instead it splatted on his pants. This was a huge mistake on my part; it was like waking a hibernating bear. He seemed to admire my courage for using wet manure yet still had to retaliate. I ran for the bus and caught in my sights a peaceful mom painting in the shade. I hated to bother her, but I was about to get clobbered. I attached myself so firmly to mom's leg that you did not know where I began and she ended.

"Matthew leave her alone and get out of here". Oh, thank gwad, I mumbled, as I looked upward to heaven.

"But she hit me with manure," he protested.

"Matthew, I don't care. Just stop, please stop."

This was an interesting observation; a person can be the aggressor and then act like he or she is the victim. Depending on the judge and jury and how tired and fed up they are and how willing they are to examine the facts determines whether justice is served or not, and life is not fair.

One weekend, we showed up at the lake with something truly spectacular—Dad had somehow acquired an authentic World War II submarine life raft. It was roughly fifteen feet long, with an inflatable arching frame covered in heavy canvas, designed to weather open-ocean storms. Inside were hand pumps for bailing water, a black inflatable floor, and pouches for rations and medical gear. It even *looked* like it meant business—bold black and orange, impossible to miss. If there had been any doubt before, this raft sealed it: *"The crazy Italians have arrived."*

I was still young enough to be impressed, not embarrassed. The older kids, on the other hand, were visibly horrified. But as Dad finished inflating it and nudged it into Lake Berryessa, the raft took to the water like a dream—this massive, floating beast, equal parts survival equipment and circus act. It drifted out with the slow majesty of James's giant peach, absurd and glorious.

Time on the lake lasted only a week or so when one cool summer Sunday it was suddenly time to load up and go home. The older kids packed up the larger things and the younger kids the smaller things. The giant orange raft took everyone to sit on it and deflate it so it would fold enough to store. With all those projects done, Dad started the Camp-a-lot, and we were on the road, back home. Not an hour into the drive, the engine quit.

"Shit," Dad called out. He pulled off to the side of the road and up went the hood, and he came back inside after a few minutes and said he needed to get to the auto parts store down the road about 5 miles. So, he walked out of the bus, put his thumb up in the air, and began walking down the highway. He just accepted it and left. It was a lesson in just dealing with it, and not bemoaning your lot in life. We sat there, parked on the side of the road hour after hour listening to the whoosh whoosh whoosh of passing cars. It wasn't more than an hour before he was back, tarp draped under the engine on the ground, parts and tools everywhere. Mom kept the coffee going, and Mike helped him until it was running again. There was no panic or anger, just, "Well, that's the way it is and we gotta deal with it."

So impressed with his quiet resolve of the situation, I went to my cubby hole and pulled out my composition book and wrote down, "When your bus breaks down, just deal with it."

She was my age, but light years ahead in poise—Princess Diana, gliding through palace corridors with a smile that masked the minefield beneath her heels. I watched her the way a girl watches a heroine: eyes wide, breath held, hoping she'd somehow win. Behind her shimmer and silk was a woman dodging icy glances from royal blood and whispering scandals from the man she married.

Chapter Three: Innovation

Searching for answers and strength, her butler once said she devoured the book called *The Road Less Traveled*. I imagined her curled on a velvet sofa, highlighter in hand, stopping cold at the first line:

"Life is difficult."

Yeah. No kidding.

That phrase—*"Life is difficult"*—hit different after Greece. We came home sun-kissed, over-packed, and semi-delusional. I was convinced we'd settle somewhere fresh. Maybe a university town. Maybe a city with a stoplight.

But Lorenzo? He got misty-eyed and said, "Let's go back to where it all began."

He meant the dusty little mining town. I thought he meant the Olive Garden in Crete. Naturally, his "new beginning" meant moving straight into his parents' house. Because what better way to reboot your life than sharing one bathroom with three generations and a collection of decorative spoons?

"It's just until we find a place," he said cheerfully, stepping over his grandma's oxygen tank.

Lorenzo's parents were a paradox. His father invited us to move in, but the stiffness in his jaw and the way his eyes flicked toward Lorenzo felt more like setting a trap to prove a point. Around the room, Lorenzo's moody brother sat slouched, barely hiding his irritation. Our toddler's high-pitched shrieks echoed off the walls, while I clutched a book, feeling their eyes on me like I was a challenge.

From the first day, I rubbed them the wrong way. My family built things—treehouses, furniture, futures—while his family talked in circles, their words grand but empty. I didn't hold back on pointing that out, again and again, watching their faces tighten like a storm ready to break.

Their house was perched alone atop a barren hill, surrounded by jagged rocks and stiff Bull Pines that creaked in the dry wind. Somewhere above, a hawk screeched as it dive-bombed a helpless desert critter, breaking the stillness. Otherwise, nothing stirred—just endless dirt, an open sky, and a quiet judgment hanging heavy in the air.

The gravel driveway snaked up to a plain sage-green two-story box, squatting like a Monopoly house dumped on the dullest patch of earth. No sheds leaned crooked. No treehouses climbed skyward. No half-finished projects cluttered the yard. Thirty years of living and not a single nail hammered—just untouched, stubborn stillness.

What kept them busy all day?

One word: football. If they weren't glued to the TV, they were tossing a ball in the yard. Pop Warner, high school Friday nights, Thanksgiving flag football, Foosball tournaments raging in the living room, and framed portraits of gridiron legends glaring down from the walls like saints in a cathedral. I hadn't just married into a family—I'd been drafted into the Football Vatican.

Lorenzo's mom, Maria, hailed from Indiana, and her soft Midwestern lilt clung to her vowels like static on polyester. She stood nearly five-foot-ten, generously padded, with a towering beehive hairdo that screamed 1957—apparently, she'd missed the memo. Her thick Coke-bottle glasses magnified her eyes to cartoonish

Chapter Three: Innovation

proportions, making her look permanently wide-eyed. I couldn't help but catch myself staring.

Her vice of choice? Dolly Madison Snowballs—pink, spongy, coconut-coated sugar clouds. She didn't just like them; she practically worshipped them. One entire cupboard was reserved for these sacred treats, sealed off with a mother's glare sharp enough to freeze time. The kids knew better than to so much as glance in that direction. That cupboard wasn't just off-limits—it was holy ground, guarded by years of growls and snack-hoarding rituals.

Maria was sweet enough in her own way. One afternoon, I sat slumped at the kitchen table, simmering with silent rage at Lorenzo for dragging me back to this godforsaken outpost. I swear, if he'd spontaneously combusted right then, I wouldn't have had the decency to spit on him to put out the flames.

Just then, Maria looked up from her Snowball, those cartoonishly magnified eyes wide with concern, and in her soft Midwestern singsong said, "Honey, you need to get outta the house. You've wershed all the laundry, the kids are fed—come on, let's go to Thrifty's."

"Why would I want to go to Thrifty's?" I asked, genuinely baffled.

Maria blinked at me, her bug-eyed glasses amplifying her sincerity. "Because we can meet people from town there. It'll be good for you."

I stared at her like she'd just beamed down from Planet Midwestern Motivation, *Meet people- Wha?"* What I thought but did not say was:

What I really wanted was simple: to go to school, have a house of my own, and a second set of wheels that didn't involve handlebars. A husband who understood that "a night out" meant more than splitting a Filet-O-Fish under fluorescent lights. A savings account—heck, maybe even some investments. And above all, I wanted to stop being branded "demanding" or "difficult" just because I aimed for a life that didn't revolve around weekly pilgrimages to the drugstore.

"No thanks, Maria," I said, shaking my head with a small smile, and headed outside to play football with my kids—two now, running circles around me.

When we weren't scouring the classifieds looking for a place of our own to live or chasing toddlers with jam-hands, we pitched in around the in-laws' house as best we could. Lorenzo would grab a hammer and start whacking away at something—usually something that didn't need it. I helped in my own special way: by pointing out the things that actually needed fixing, often with the enthusiasm of a foreman who'd lost her crew.

One bright Saturday afternoon, we were gathered around the kitchen table—me, Lorenzo, and our crumb-dusted little duo—eating sandwiches and trying to keep the applesauce from hitting the curtains. Out of nowhere, Maria came thundering up the stairs, panting and wild-eyed like she'd just discovered gold.

"Kids! Kids! Come see what your dad has built!"

Accidentally dropping my plastic fork into Maria's ashtray, I sighed, scooped up the kids, and followed her downstairs.

She led us to the corner of the front room and began swooning—literally swooning—over Grandpa's latest creation. "Aaaah! Look at this! He built it himself!" she beamed.

Chapter Three: Innovation

There it stood: a *bookshelf*. Three pieces of wood balanced across six concrete cinder blocks, all spray-painted a shiny, uneven black. Lorenzo's little sister—maybe thirteen—and his two teenage brothers gathered around, offering up synchronized gasps like they were witnessing the Sistine Chapel.

It was the third piece of furniture in the room, joining the infamous red couch (its rips patched with gray duct tape) and the three-legged coffee table, heroically propped up with more cinder blocks. The bookshelf, I noticed, held exactly zero books.

Confused, I laughed—honestly thinking it was a gag. "Wow. Are you kidding me? That is... crap. Okay, you've got a *gift*, my friend—good one. So, where's the real one?"

Silence. The kind of silence that sucks the air right out of a room. Turns out, that *was* the real one. And apparently, it was his *masterpiece*. I stared at the floor, mortified. Ashamed of my insensitivity, yes—but also deeply, existentially depressed. What was I doing? Living in a house with no books, married to a man who thought duct tape was interior design, surrounded by people who clapped for cinder blocks?

Things did start looking up—though not in the way you'd expect. One explosive dinner, two slammed doors, and three days of frosty silence later, Maria stood at the edge of the living room, arms crossed, lips pursed, and announced, "We found you a place." Eight miles down the road, they drove us to a trailer park. But Ed, ever chipper, patted the side of the rusty single-wide and declared, "Best deal in town. The park looks drug-free—far as I could tell driving by."

I doubted he'd slowed down long enough to spot anything but the "For Rent" sign, but I nodded. At that point, even a shack with plumbing felt like deliverance.

They handed over the keys without ceremony. No hugs. No guilt trips. And best of all, no more pressure to call them Mom and Dad. Just "Maria" and "Ed" now, like we were coworkers at a DMV. I could've wept from the sheer relief.

Later that night, I stood barefoot on the trailer's cold linoleum, watching Lorenzo wrestle a wobbly table leg into submission while the kids scattered crayons across the floor.

This was it. Not perfect. Not even decent. But ours. If life was a mess of problems, maybe it was time to grab a rag and start scrubbing. I'd keep the peace. Be agreeable. Smaller, if I had to be. My in-laws could have the spotlight. I just wanted a little room to breathe.

Over time, our relationship simmered into something volatile—like one of those old pressure cookers with the metal knob, jittering on the stove, whispering warnings no one seemed to hear. Visits to their house became silent auditions, where every word I uttered—or swallowed—was met with squints and sideways glances. I'd say "thank you," and somehow it meant, "I'm better than you." I'd stay quiet, and that meant judgment. They twisted my words into balloon animals I didn't recognize, then popped them with glee.

It didn't matter what I meant. They'd already cast me: the outsider. The interloper. That Catholic girl from the wrong side of their expectations. Their suspicion settled in like dust in a neglect-

Chapter Three: Innovation

ed corner—hard to notice at first, but impossible to get rid of. And somewhere along the way, I stopped trying.

I began to dread their voices, their smirks, the way Maria clutched her pearls every time I mentioned Mass. Their coldness became a mirror, and I started to reflect it. I hardened. Pulled back. Let the gap between us grow until it echoed. If they wanted a reason to keep me at arm's length, I'd give it to them. Different? Fine. Too much? Absolutely. Catholic enough to never quite fit in? Amen. And somehow, that made it easier. And sadder.

Life in the trailer wasn't exactly a fresh start. The tension still hummed beneath the surface—low and steady, like a leaky gas line no one wanted to admit smelling. We weren't just different; we were chemically incompatible. Oil and water. Cats and vacuum cleaners.

One hot and sticky afternoon, I stood in the weed-pocked yard, gesturing toward the rusted satellite dish and plastic flamingo with hope in my voice. "What if we planted some flowers? Maybe a little stone path? Something to make it feel like home?"

Lorenzo wrapped his arms around me from behind, kissed my neck, and said, "Honey, your beauty is beauty enough for this garden."

I laughed—because what else could I do? The weeds laughed too, still firmly in place.

A few days later, I brought up the fact that we did not own a vacuum. "We really need one."

He looked up from the couch, where he was digging into a bowl of dry cereal.

"What for? Vacuums are overrated. We've got a perfectly good broom." His barely understandable reply came with a smack, smack, smack.

"For the carpet?" I stared at him like he'd just suggested we churn our own butter.

He shrugged. That was Lorenzo's specialty—shrugging things into nonexistence.

The following Sunday, we were halfway out the door to church when he noticed our five-year-old son's sweater was matted with dog hair.

Lorenzo scowled. "He looks terrible."

I pointed at the carpet, still embedded with our German shepherd's winter coat. "Well, you said we didn't need a vacuum."

He paused, blinked, then nodded like a benevolent king. "Right. Okay, get one tomorrow."

"Oh, gee. Thanks."

Figuring I was on a roll, I eased down beside him, picking my moment like a secret weapon. "The tires," I said softly, "they're bald. Really bald."

He didn't look up at first—just kept munching cereal. Finally, he met my eyes with a solemn nod. "I've been reading about being greener consumers. Reduce. Reuse." He tapped his chin seriously. "So, I figure we wait until the cords show."

The cords. Inside the tires.

I sank back into the cushion, biting back the urge to roll my eyes. Instead, I just listened to the pressure cooker lid inside my mind starting its faint rattle again. I skipped the fight and took the car to the tire shop myself.

Chapter Three: Innovation

Tired of begging for something as basic as safety, I felt more like a lone ambassador married to a foreign exchange student than a partner. Divorce crept into my thoughts—heavy words for a Catholic, a marriage that's supposed to be a sacrament, a vow. Plenty of women had it worse, I told myself. At least, I wasn't bruised. That was my line in the sand: unbruised.

So, I stayed. But I changed direction. I pushed for buying a house, getting us out of the trailer park. Maybe a new address would shift the broken pieces. Maybe. I hoped. I prayed.

After months of pushing this boulder uphill—otherwise known as my husband—we finally snagged a modest win: a cozy 900-square-foot house perched on a hill, complete with a scruffy little yard. The last one in the county under a hundred grand, no less. Somehow, by scraping together every penny, we managed a $9,000 deposit and called it ours.

For a while, I found a rhythm. I enrolled in community college and made pilgrimages to the library—my sanctuary—stuffing my brain with anything that wasn't dinner, laundry, or Lorenzo. The silence of books was a kinder soundtrack than the chaos at home.

But peace never stuck around long. The car began its slow collapse. Being, essentially, a married "alone person," I did what any self-respecting abandoned woman would: I dove headfirst into research. Books on car loans, Kelley Blue Book values, Consumer Reports—how to fix cars, buy cars, negotiate cars, and spot a salesman before he flashed his artificially white teeth.

Armed with a paper avalanche of books, printouts and notes, I marched into the kitchen and dumped it all on the table like a manifesto of empowerment.

"Sit," I said. Lorenzo did—briefly. He flipped through a few pages, nodded at a chart, then popped open a beer and settled back. We "read" together. I skimmed comparison charts; he sipped, punctuating with the occasional belch. Each beer burp floated across the table like Morse code for *I'm not actually doing this.*

He wasn't reading. He was playing along.

The next day, he proved it. He pulled into the driveway behind the wheel of a Jeep Wagoneer Laredo—a clunky 2.5-liter engine that couldn't push a Radio Flyer up a hill, let alone a family. A quick scan of my well-worn Consumer Reports confirmed it: one of the worst-rated models on the market. Classic.

After four days of not speaking to him, I finally grabbed the keys and drove the Jeep to the grocery store, which was perched inconveniently on a steep hill. Loaded up the groceries, hit the highway, and started the uphill slog. I floored the gas pedal. Nothing. The engine groaned as if being asked to perform a miracle. Traffic hovered on my bumper like they were auditioning for a demolition derby.

I felt like Fred Flintstone—feet out the bottom, pedaling for my life in a prehistoric tin can. I even rocked forward and backward, forward and backward, like a madwoman, hoping momentum would help. I finally coaxed it to a heroic 35 mph, just in time to earn honks, tailgates, and a symphony of angry gestures. I screeched into the driveway, dumped the keys on the table, and said flatly, "Take it back."

Two hours later, Lorenzo stumbled in drunk and slurred, "They won't take it back."

Chapter Three: Innovation

Marching back to the library, dread riding shotgun, I found my answer, sure enough, buried in the fine print of the Federal Trade Commission's cooling-off rule: you only get three days for a no-questions-asked return. After that?

You're screwed.

And we were.

What would Scott Peck do? I reached for my battered copy of *The Road Less Traveled*—its pages swollen and stained from beer condensation, courtesy of Lorenzo's makeshift coaster habits. I flipped to the chapter on love and responsibility, hoping for some divine insight or at least a nudge toward sanity.

Peck writes: *"It is the whole process of meeting and solving problems that life has meaning. Problems are the cutting edge that distinguishes between success and failure. Problems call forth our courage and our wisdom; indeed, they create our courage and our wisdom. It is only because of problems that we grow mentally and spiritually. It is through the pain of confronting and resolving problems that we learn."*

I closed the book and muttered under my breath, "Okay, Scott... but what if you're married to the problem?"

Owning that Jeep was like dating a moody, unreliable boyfriend—constant drama, zero respect. One afternoon, groceries packed tight, it just died. I pulled over, popped the hood, and fiddled with the cooling hoses like a roadside MacGyver.

Next day, thermostat got swapped. It behaved... for a minute. Then came the familiar knocking, like a bad joke you can't escape.

Then the pothole. Tires thudded hard, groceries flew like startled birds. Eggs? Sacrificed on the dashboard altar.

I pulled over, grumbling, when smoke puffed out like the Jeep was signaling surrender. Cars honked, one guy yelled, "Hey, lady, Your car's on fire!"

Shouting back at him, "Thanks, Captain Obvious."

Steam poured from the radiator—and I remembered Dad, calm as a cucumber, fixing our busted bus on the roadside. No fuss, he just began doing what needed to be done. That example he set came marching back: Just deal with it. So, I did.

I killed the engine, stepped out of the vehicle and scanned the horizon, drew a long, deep breath of clean mountain air. The morning sun spilled over the ridge, casting golden shadows through the oaks. In a clearing, a small herd of horses grazed—some still, some prancing, one playfully chasing another. Raw, wild, untamed.

It was the kind of beauty I'd forgotten existed, and in that quiet moment, something clicked. My mind wandered back to Camp-a-lot. To Warwick Castle. To King Arthur and the quiet unraveling of everything he loved.

"Left heartbroken, Arthur mourned not only his marriage and friendship but his fractured kingdom. Doubt crept in—could a realm born of such imperfection survive in a world so prone to falling?"

That question had come back to me—again and again. I'd been wrestling with the Jeep, but really, I was the one falling apart. Catholic life had taught me that endurance was a virtue—suffer with grace. But this? This wasn't grace. This was erasure.

It was time to be honest. In the words of Aristotle: *"Plato is dear to me, but dearer still is truth."*

Chapter Three: Innovation

And the truth settled over me like a storm rolling in from the horizon—slow at first, then sudden and suffocating. Lorenzo wasn't just a weekend drunk. He was a full-time alcoholic. No rehab. No reckoning. No fairy tale ending. And yet, somehow, that brutal truth didn't crush me. It steadied me. Gave me clarity. In its strange, unwelcome way—it gave me a kind of superpower.

Why is it called the road less traveled? Because most people would rather binge-watch reality TV than face the ugly stuff. But problems? They don't disappear. They lurk like potholes waiting to swallow you whole.

There I was again, shrinking—grinning like a sitcom star, playing helpless just to keep the in-laws off my back. Enough. I wiped off the fake smile, cracked my knuckles, and got ready to stand up, even if it ruffled feathers.

First thing's first—I was flipping the whole script. For me, for the kids, starting *now*.

Lorenzo had my copy of *The Road Less Traveled*, the steady wife, and the roof. If he wanted to keep all that, discipline was on *his* to-do list.

Next: sell the damn Jeep before it broke me. Step three: face the mountain of repair bills. My plan? Drop out of school, grab a job, and actually adult.

That afternoon crawled like a snail on sedatives while I waited for Lorenzo's prison guard shift to end. When he finally walked in, I laid it out: Jeep? Gone. School? Bye-bye. Work? Bring it on.

His Oscar-worthy reaction?

"Um, okay. Whatever you want."

I said, "And I need the truck for the library run. Oh, and watch the kids."

He popped open a beer, flopped on the couch, and deadpanned, "I'm okay with that."

Driving up to the county library instantly lowered my blood pressure—it was the one place that actually made sense in the chaos of my life. Honestly, it should be renamed the Building of Answers. I wandered the aisles until a book title jumped out at me: *Clan of the Cave Bear* by Jean Auel.

I grabbed it without hesitation and dived into the story of Ayla, a five-year-old blond-haired, blue-eyed girl who survives a catastrophic earthquake only to be orphaned and badly hurt. She gets taken in by a tribe of Neanderthals—gruff, dour, and cold—which, frankly, reminded me a lot of my in-laws. Despite their huge physical and intellectual differences, they choose to raise this peculiar, sensitive, and intelligent child.

But, naturally, Ayla's uniqueness rubs everyone the wrong way. Her "husband," Broud—brutal and unforgiving, much like a certain Lorenzo—makes her life miserable, pushing her to plan a daring escape from their oppressive world.

The story hit a little too close to home, so I wisely put the book back on the shelf before it got me in trouble.

Then, right there in the lobby, I spotted a bulletin board ad: the local sheriff's department was hiring. The only requirements? Be able to run fast and have no felonies. Jackpot. I thought, "That's me."

Chapter Three: Innovation

The very next day, I applied. Four months later, I was hired and officially became a Deputy Sheriff, a title that felt like a new chapter in a very complicated book.

Chapter Four

Playing with the Boys

An eight-foot-deep kidney-shaped pool became the center of our chlorine-scented summers when the family was not traveling. Dressed in a pink swimsuit with a frilly bottom, flip-flops clacking on the concrete, the shimmering water beckoned me.

One summer, Marc was lying atop one of the raft mats—dragged from the old World War II life raft—basking in the sun like a satisfied otter, pleased with his own ingenuity. I slipped into the shallow end and swam around, joined by Little Andy and Vince. We settled in to play, the sun warming our skin, the water perfectly comfortable. We challenged each other to see who could hold their breath the longest.

Drawn by the giant raft covering half the pool, we swam up to join Marc. He made room, and the four of us sat together, peacefully listening to the gentle *lap, lap, lap* of the water.

Then—*splash!*—a huge cannonball disrupted the quiet. Blaise had jumped in the pool. We froze, watching him like we'd just spotted a shark. Surprisingly, he stayed calm—that is, at least until Marc left.

"Oh, don't leave, Marc!" we pleaded. But he'd had enough and was heading inside to call his girlfriend. That left the three of us—Little Andy, Vince, and me—alone in the water with the Shark.

Blaise.

Chapter Four: Playing with the Boys

I don't think Dad was around enough to properly socialize him. Blaise never really learned how to read the room—or the pool. He didn't understand boundaries, his own or anyone else's. He'd push too hard, play too rough, and never realize that when things got out of hand, the game ended—not just that day, but over and over again. We'd leave, and he'd be alone, which only seemed to fuel his frustration and fire.

Today was no different. Blaise got that wild glint in his eye and decided we were playing *King of the Mat*. Only *he* ever really wanted to play that game; we certainly did not. He was always the roughest, playing like it was a death match, even when the rest of us just wanted to float.

The rules were simple: the person on the raft had to be knocked off. But when Blaise was King, it took all three of us to even stand a chance. Alone, none of us was a match.

"Blaise, let me on," I said, treading water beside the edge.

He grinned—meanly—and growled, "Ha ha ha, no," before planting his hand squarely on my face and shoving me under.

On this went, Little Andy, Vince, and I each getting shoved. There were waves in the pool splashing so high that the concrete sidewalk around the pool was drench. The pad was so wide and huge that I got shoved under it. Running out of oxygen and feeling panic take over, I picked a direction and kept going until I was out from under the air mattress pad of death. Gasping for air, I hauled myself up out of the pool. I thought to myself.... "He cannot keep this going, tormenting us, and we cannot keep going to mom. He will just do something when she is not looking. We must get some kind of control of this nut."

And then I had an idea.

As Little Andy hauled himself out of the water like a soggy, defeated rat, Vince climbed out behind him, shaking like a wet noodle.

"Guys, listen," I whispered urgently. "We have to take him down—together."

Little Andy and Vince leaned in.

"Andy, we'll make it look like you're giving up. I'll rip up this white towel—we'll all wave it, pretend we're surrendering. Then, while he's distracted, Vince and I will come in from the corners of the raft and push up with everything we've got."

Andy nodded, already grinning.

"'K?"

"'K."

Vince, the group's resident justice warrior, declared with total seriousness, "Yeah, and after we knock him off, we dump the mud pie on his head." To Vince, Blaise wasn't just a kid—he was the neighborhood dictator, and injustice was personal.

I warned him, "Not a great idea, Vince. We'll get in trouble for dirtying the pool." He grudgingly agreed. And just like that, our plan was set in motion.

Timmy slid into the water like a miniature dolphin—quick and smooth for a six-year-old. He popped up by the raft, waving a torn white towel like a surrender flag, shouting, "Blaise, Blaise, I quit. Can I come up?"

"Okay, Andy," came the response, "Just say, 'Blaise is the king of the pool,' and you can come up."

Chapter Four: Playing with the Boys

Little Andy nailed it, eyes wide with perfectly fake admiration: "Blaise is the king of the pool."

While Andy flattered the tyrant, Vince and I slipped silently into the water. Unnoticed, we took deep breaths, dove like covert commandos to opposite corners of the raft, screamed our best underwater war cries,

"Light of Albion, guide my hand," and pushed with everything we had.

The raft exploded upward, launching both boys into the air. In a flash, Vince and I scrambled on top, whooping with joy. Vince reached down, pulled Little Andy up, and we all collapsed onto the mat in victory.

We had done it. *We had taken the raft.*

The celebration didn't last long. Blaise, furious and freakishly strong, clambered back aboard and dumped us all like yesterday's laundry.

Still, we didn't care. For a few glorious minutes, we had vanquished the dragon.

Knowing full well how vengeful Blaise could be, we didn't wait around. We made a break for it—sprinting to the house and slamming the door behind us and locking it. Locking the doors was a big thing in our house.

Running through the living room, I passed mom and her friend from church, Alice, discussing stockpiling supplies for the end of the world, "Gold Krugerrands, and Toilet Paper," they both nodded in agreement. Skidding past them on my way to the kitchen, I thought on this for a brief moment, "What about food?"

When I got to the kitchen, Vince and Little Andy were already hard at work, pulling out the peanut butter and jelly like seasoned survivors. Meanwhile, outside, Blaise was pounding on the door and yowling, "Let me in—let me *in!*"

We ignored him, of course—and began inching ourselves and our sandwiches closer to Mom at the end of the table, our expressions carefully neutral.

"Becca, go let your brother in," she snapped, without even looking at me—still smiling sweetly at Alice.

"Fine," I muttered, stomping off. I unlocked the door, then executed a perfect serpentine sprint back to the kitchen—zig, zag, *dive!*—just as Blaise lunged. His swipe missed me by a hair, literally, and instead grazed the ends of Mom's carefully set curls.

A collective gasp burst out from the kitchen like a holy wind.

He'd hit Mom's hair. *Mom's hair!*

It was like someone had just taken a swing at the Pope.

"Blaise, you get in your room right now and don't come out until I tell you to." Mom smiled at Alice and said, "Would you like some more coffee?"

Wow, this worked out better than any of us three had planned. Unfortunately, there is no statute of limitations for revenge, and we knew Blaise would have it. Yet it was comforting to know that this would not come for many hours since mom had a way of forgetting who she had banished to their rooms throughout the day.

Parade days turned the old school bus into box seats at the Rose Bowl. Parked just right along the curb—thanks to Dad's uncanny knack for snagging prime real estate—our rig transformed into a double-decker viewing stand. Those welded pipe stairs

Chapter Four: Playing with the Boys

clanked under the weight of excited feet scrambling up to the plywood roof deck. A blanket thrown down, maybe a cooler perched nearby, and suddenly we were royalty watching our subjects pass.

Then came the band—*our* band. And leading the charge: Marc.

Out in front like a general on parade, he could've passed for West Point brass—if West Point issued gold braid and shiny buttons to teenagers with acne. His tall hat bobbed as he marched, that massive white feather wagging like it had opinions of its own. The crowd leaned in. Every move was crisp, deliberate—the strut, the spin, the reverse walk, the perfect toss of the mace high into the blue. Not a flinch, not a fumble. That thing sailed, twirled, landed squarely in his palm like gravity was on his payroll.

Behind him, the band followed like they knew they were part of something glorious. And in that moment, with the sunlight gleaming off that shiny uniform and the crowd eating it up, Marc wasn't just leading the band. He *was* the parade.

The streets buzzed with bodies and brass—locals and out-of-towners shoulder to shoulder, squinting into the sun and jockeying for a better view. Folding chairs claimed curbs like squatters. Babies dozed in strollers, teenagers loitered in clusters, and the scent of kettle corn tangled with something unmistakably... beer.

It was a big parade—*the* big one—and folks came from every dusty corner of Northern California to either march in it or drink like they had.

Bars kept their doors wide open, music spilling out along with a few staggered patrons. One such wanderer, plastic cup in hand and sunglasses too big for his face, weaved through the crowd like a boat listing in shallow water. He ambled up to the bus—the big brown beast that served as our portable grandstand—and took a long, squinty look at the painted letters running down its side.

"Caaaamp...uhhh...lottttttt," he read, dragging each syllable like he was trying to land a plane on a gravel runway. His steps brought him to the window where Mom sat, fanning herself.

His eyes landed on her and widened like he'd just stumbled into a wildlife documentary. "Holy sheet," he announced, voice full of wonder and beer. "It's a whole *fookin'* family in here!"

Mom's fan hit the floor. She jolted upright like the seat had turned electric and shrieked, "Oh, *Andy!*"

But Dad was already moving—half smirk, all calm. He appeared at the bus door like a magician's assistant and slid down to the curb, one hand casually on the drunk's back, the other already pointing under the hood. Didn't take long before the guy was nodding like he understood a word of what Dad was saying about engines, hands stuffed in his pockets, happy as a clam—completely unaware he'd just scared the life out of a mother who nearly climbed out the window to chase him off with a shoe.

After what felt like three full parades and a minor sunburn, the familiar beat of "Tusk" came rolling down the street, carried on the backs of tubas and teenage sweat. Heads turned. There they were—Marc's high school marching band, finally in sight, every kid in step and gleaming like a row of toy soldiers fresh out of the box.

Marc had drilled them for months, probably in his sleep, too, and it showed. From the first blast of brass to the clean snap of each turn, they nailed it. Right out front, there he was—our Marc—commanding the street in his tall hat and gold cords like some musical field general.

Chapter Four: Playing with the Boys

Mom beamed so hard it was a wonder her sunglasses didn't melt. Every time someone leaned over to say how sharp Marc looked, how tight the band sounded, she'd practically burst. "Yes, he's a Major!" she'd gush.

"Oh?" they'd ask, eyebrows climbing. "What branch of the military?"

Dad, standing nearby with his arms folded and a knowing smile, would clear it up without missing a beat. "Drum Major. She means Drum Major."

But Mom's enthusiasm had a way of outrunning her accuracy. Like when Marc was elected president of the local Catholic youth group—CCD. She told everyone he'd been chosen to lead the CIA.

"Oooh," folks would nod, wide-eyed. "And he's *so* young!"

Marc wasn't always heaven's favorite. In fact, on this particular trip, his halo was noticeably missing. Mom, worn slick from a long day of sun, sweat, and small talk, had slumped into her seat without so much as a headcount. She gave Dad the go-ahead wave with one hand while the other rubbed slow circles into her temples—classic sign of a woman who had fielded one too many "Where's the bathroom?" questions.

Unbeknownst to her, a secret mission was already underway.

As the last tuba was being loaded into its case and the crowd started to thin, Marc, Paul, and Blaise quietly broke formation and made a beeline for the ladder bolted to the back of the bus—the one that led to the rooftop parade platform.

"Where are you guys going?" The words left my mouth before I even knew I was ratting.

Marc leaned in like he was inviting me to knock over a casino. "Up the ladder. Up to the top. Wanna come?"

He didn't need to ask twice. I would've eaten a bug for Marc just to stay in his orbit. But riding on top of a moving school bus? That was next-level rebellion. The kind of stunt that came with real risk—parental wrath, asphalt rash, possible eternal damnation. Still, the way he said it made it sound like an adventure no sane kid could refuse.

So, I said yes.

And up we went, chasing trouble one rung at a time.

Legs kept climbing, even as the brain screamed, *Stay, you idiot—STAY*. But by the time that warning finished echoing around my skull, I was already wedged between Marc and Paul on top of the bus, lying flat on a nest of old sleeping bags like a trio of roof-riding fugitives.

Fingers clamped onto the copper railing—six measly inches of tubing that, during parades, had always felt sturdy enough. The bus rumbled to life beneath us. At five miles an hour, it was quaint. At fifty? It suddenly felt more like decoration than safety feature. My knuckles turned ghost-white, sweat pooling in my palms, heartbeat somewhere near my ears.

The plywood deck shook slightly as tires rolled out, and for a split second I imagined it tearing off entirely like a carnival ride gone rogue. But when I glanced sideways, Marc and Paul weren't scared, they were grinning. Wide, wild, fearless grins.

And then came the onramp.

As the bus picked up speed, a collective loud roar burst from the boys—pure, reckless joy. That kind of sound only comes from

Chapter Four: Playing with the Boys

the young and the stupid, and at that moment, we were both. Wind in our faces, wheels humming below, it felt like flying—illegal, thrilling, idiotic flying.

Then the turn.

Off the freeway almost as fast as we'd gotten on, the bus jerked to a stop on the shoulder, brakes hissing like a snake ready to strike.

The doors swung open.

And out stepped Dad.

Barrel-chested, red-faced, all-Italian thunder.

"What the HELL are you kids doing up there?! Get down! NOW!"

The joy died instantly. We scrambled for the ladder like rats from a sinking ship, praying our legs moved faster than Dad's temper.

Dad planted himself at the bottom of the ladder, eyes locked on Marc, Paul, and Blaise as they clumsily scrambled down, one by one. Just as he was about to unleash the storm, my head popped up from behind the bus roof like a surprised meerkat.

"You, too?" he growled, disbelief thick in his voice.

"For God's sake," he barked, shaking his head. "You had your little sister up there? Stupid, stupid, stupid."

One by one, whack! —backs of their heads met Dad's heavy hand as they shuffled back onto the bus, tails tucked. I braced myself, flinching in anticipation of my turn to get the classic whack, but it never came.

That night, I pulled out my notebook and wrote it all down. Sometimes, it turns out, you don't need someone else to whack you to know you've been stupid — you're perfectly capable of doing it to yourself. Hard enough, too.

Not exactly the job that had been dreamed of, but when life hands out only a handful of lemons, lemonade becomes the priority—whether sweetened or sour. College was on pause, shelved like an unfinished book, because now the real world was knocking hard, and there was no going back to the safety of home or playing with babies. This new world demanded survival skills—skills sharper than a baby's cry and far more complex.

Workplace politics, a phrase never heard before, suddenly loomed large, a puzzle no one had warned about. The police academy came with a motto that stuck like gum on a boot: *Adapt and Overcome.* Those words echoed in every grueling lesson that followed, hard and fast.

The rough-and-tumble playtime with brothers? Maybe more useful than anyone had guessed—practice for a world dominated by men and their unwritten rules.

For a flicker of inspiration, my eyes drifted to Winston Churchill's *The World Crisis*—only to recoil at six intimidating volumes staring back like a staring contest from history. That ambition got shelved quicker than the college plan.

Still, Churchill's name lingered—a symbol of sharp strategy and the kind of leadership that could move mountains. Maybe it was premature to dive into epic tomes just yet. Better to see what

Chapter Four: Playing with the Boys

the Sheriff's Department had to teach first. Then, perhaps, the right book to guide the way would reveal itself.

Weaponry, first lesson: I needed to purchase my own gun because the Department was too poor to assign one. I'd shopped for dresses before but never for a gun—this was a first-time experience. Parking in front of Bullseye Bargain Outlet, I stepped through the door, setting off a little bell that tinkled sharply in the quiet store.

The clerk behind the counter was huge and intimidating—a good-looking fella, too. His dark eyes pinned me like a hawk. I quickly looked away, feeling suddenly small.

"Can I help you?" came his gruff voice, low and rough like gravel.

"Ah, yes," I replied, fumbling for confidence. "Um, well, I, uh, was just hired as a Deputy Sheriff, and I was told I could purchase a gun here." My voice wavered despite my effort to sound steady. The weight of the moment pressed on me—this wasn't just a transaction. It felt like a test.

He glanced at me, then swept his gaze over the walls lined with guns—shining metal, cold steel, deadly shapes—and back at me again. Making a sucking sound with his mouth, he licked his teeth and said, "Name's Balls. First name Harry. Follow me."

Next lesson: these people are sarcastic, with a dry sense of humor. I thought, *that can't possibly be his real name.*

Some things you learn by knowing without knowing. In the world of weaponry, you have to prove yourself to be accepted. They don't care if you look like you belong or not. **PROVE IT** is their silent challenge. Pretenders are sniffed out and dismissed; honesty and humility earn respect.

Because I was utterly ignorant about guns, Harry picked out a Smith & Wesson 9mm for me. "Fits your hands," he said gruffly, "and the recoil won't knock you on your ass."

He explained recoil as the backward force that pushes the gun against your hand when the bullet fires forward. His voice was casual, but the concept sent a ripple of unease through me.

When I held the gun, it was surprisingly heavy, a cold weight that settled deeply in my palm. The grip was hard plastic, patterned with sharp diamond cuts that dug into my skin, reminding me this was no toy. The cold metal barrel glinted under the fluorescent lights, a silent promise of power and danger.

My thumb rested on a small metal loop at the top, and my fingers curled naturally around the thick grip. It felt oddly tailored, designed to fit perfectly, to be wielded like an extension of my own body.

That a tool meant to kill could feel so comfortable was a paradox that gnawed at me.

My mind started to race. *Fire? Shoot?* He had no idea who I was. I could've been some unhinged lunatic, a suburban *Basic Instinct* just waiting for a chance to go full Sharon Stone—and here he was, just handing me a loaded weapon? No background check, no psyche eval, not even a blood pressure reading?

So, we're really doing this? Just... hand out guns to whoever walks in off the street? Is that how this works? I glanced down at the 9mm in my hands, absurdly aware that they'd only ever cradled

Chapter Four: Playing with the Boys

babies, balanced sippy cups, and once, a bowl of Jell-O shaped like a lamb for Easter. And now... this?

I don't know anything about killing people, I thought. *I still feel guilty stepping on ants.*

"Fire!" Harry barked in my ear, shattering my inner monologue like glass.

My whole body jolted. My finger, traitorous and twitchy, dropped instinctively to the trigger. Bang.

The sound cracked through the air like a whip, and the force jarred up through my arms. I blinked, disoriented. My ears rang. I felt a rush of adrenaline—or maybe shame—flood through me. I had just fired a gun. I had *actually* fired a gun.

And yet, somehow, I couldn't shake the weird feeling that this whole shooting experience was loaded with an undercurrent of something... oddly sexual. The heat, the body contact, the heavy breathing. His huge arms had encircled me like a scene straight out of a bad romance novel: *Steel and Flesh—A Firearm Love Story*. I was clearly missing a layer of meaning that everyone else here was in on.

But I went with it. Ever the eager student. Even if I had absolutely no idea what I was learning.

"Nice shot!" Harry called out.

Then, after a pause, "Other guy's target, but nice shot."

"...Thank you, Mr. Balls," I replied, with all the dignity I could muster.

My heart soared, I had fired my first bullet, ah, round that is, and from that moment I was empowered. I knew I could do this cop thing, smelly men and all.

I started working at the county jail, a facility that held fewer than 250 inmates. I quickly learned that jail isn't just one thing—it's a revolving door for all kinds of people: some waiting for court hearings, some waiting to be transferred to prison, others booked and released the same day like they were popping in for a dental cleaning. Then there were the work-release inmates, the ones who left during the day to go into the city and hold down jobs, returning at night like oddly punctual vampires. Every six months we had a shift pick, a process that felt part strategy, part blood sport. I chose the graveyard shift—it worked best for me and the family, even if it meant defying everything human biology stands for. It's no small thing, teaching your body to live backwards. But I figured it out. I blacked out the bedroom windows with layers of tin foil like I was prepping for a nuclear blast, turned on a box fan for white noise, and tried to trick my brain into thinking 2 p.m. was midnight. It wasn't glamorous, but it worked. Mostly. The hardest part wasn't the sleep, but the strangeness of living opposite the rest of the world, like I'd stepped into a secret shadow society. While other people were sipping morning coffee and walking their dogs, I was logging headcounts and confiscating shanks made out of toothbrushes.

Most nights on the job were a long, slow exercise in creative time-killing. The real entertainment usually came courtesy of the holding cells—and the characters inside them. Take Zorn, for instance. A local legend in his own right, town drunk by reputation, picked up like clockwork every week by city PD for his mandatory detox tour.

Chapter Four: Playing with the Boys

Zorn hated cops. Passionately. But only when he was drunk, which was almost always.

Standard protocol: dump him in the padded cell so he wouldn't bash his head in while ranting about government conspiracies and how the police were secretly lizard people. He'd sprawl out on the floor, face pressed close to the concrete, eyes locked on the two-inch gap beneath the cell door. It became his stage.

Whenever a pair of boots passed by, his cue line would erupt: "You motherf$#%&* donut-eating fascists! I'm not drunk!"

Then he'd promptly pass out mid-sentence, snoring like a lawnmower on its last legs—until the next pair of boots strolled past. Like clockwork, he'd come back to life and restart the show, word for word. Honestly, he was more consistent than the radio.

Although the guys I worked with weren't my brothers, they had that same mischievous energy—equal parts troublemaker and ten-year-old class clown. It was a kind of humor you couldn't fake, and frankly, it kept the place from turning into a complete mental institution.

One slow night, Rich got a wild idea. He pulled off his boots and set them just outside Zorn's padded cell door, soles pointed inward like someone was standing guard. Then he tiptoed back to the office in his socks, flopped into his chair, and propped his feet up like he'd just invented comedy.

My job? Walk past the cell in *my* boots to trigger Zorn's routine. So, I did.

Sure enough, Zorn sprang to life like a drunk Jack-in-the-box, spotted the boots, and let loose. "You mother—! I see you, you donut-sucking pigs! I ain't drunk!"

But this time, the boots didn't move. No reply. Just two empty leather sentinels standing their ground. That didn't stop Zorn. He kept right on cussing—at the boots. Loud, slurred, heartfelt.

Eventually, his rant lost steam, like a wind-up toy winding down, until he gave himself a final slurred insult and passed clean out, dead quiet.

We absolutely howled. It was juvenile. It was wrong. It was definitely not in the law enforcement handbook—and I was pretty sure I'd be confessing it by Sunday. But Lord help me, it was funny.

Friday nights had a distinct vibe—*let the games begin.* It was like the drunk Olympics. Holding cells packed out like concert venues, the receiving garage backed up with patrol vehicles from every branch imaginable: Forest Rangers, Highway Patrol, Sheriff's Office, City Police. Like a bizarre parade of uniforms, all unloading cuffed-up contestants from the evening's bad decisions.

It ran like a chaotic assembly line—one by one, the perps shuffled in: loud, slurring, weepy, belligerent, or just weirdly calm. Deputies lined up at stations, patting down pockets stuffed with lighters, loose change, gum wrappers, and the occasional mystery pill. Fingerprinting ink smudged everywhere. The air buzzed with the sharp tang of alcohol, sweat, and something no cleaning product could ever quite kill.

Out in the city, porch lights were flicking off, kids tucked in, pets curled up by the couch. But inside our fluorescent-lit underworld, a whole different city came alive—drunk, disheveled, loud and smelly.

Most were men, and most were loud—screaming, pounding fists against glass walls like drunken zoo animals at feeding time.

Chapter Four: Playing with the Boys

One guy paced in circles, shouting, "Come on! I can take you all! I don't know Karate, but I *do* know Ka-ra-zee!" He bowed at the end like he was headlining in Vegas.

Another one wouldn't shut up about being denied the sacred ritual of "walking the white line"—a field sobriety test that, according to him, was his constitutional right and also the one thing that would've proven his undeniable innocence.

After half an hour of his squawking, Rich had enough. He yanked the guy out of the cell and marched him to the beginning of the intake hallway, a dull stretch of solid gray concrete. No white lines. No yellow lines. Not a single stripe or marking anywhere. Just floor.

"Alright," Rich said, arms crossed. "Walk the line."

The guy blinked. "Okay… uh… where is it?"

"Exactly," Rich said, deadpan. "You can't see it. Because you're drunk."

And with that, he spun him around and tossed him back in the cell like a sack of bad ideas. The man sat down quietly after that, defeated by an imaginary line.

Some folks just sobered up in holding and were released with a sigh and a citation. Others got housed—processed, uniformed, and assigned a bunk like they were checking into the world's worst Airbnb.

Along the way, I got a crash course in a whole new vocabulary. Words I had *never* heard in Sunday school. One of them—let's just say it starts with "C"—was so foreign to me I tried to look it up in the dictionary. Not much luck there. Webster's was no help, so I did what any confused adult does in a pinch: I asked Lorenzo, who by then was working as a prison guard and knew more about profanity than a sailor in a traffic jam.

Sometimes, he'd just stare at me in horror, like he couldn't decide whether to laugh or cry. I don't know what he expected—I was working in a jail, for crying out loud. Did he think I was spending my nights learning French?

And so, another lesson from the grand old school of life: what truly bad words meant. Not the stuff they censor on network TV. The real ones. The ones that hit like a slap and made even grown men flinch. Turns out, language is just as much a weapon in jail as anything else.

Every week, like clockwork, we got a few "fighters." That was the only thing that could make the deputies move fast—like, Olympic-relay fast.

The booking clerk would crackle over the radio: "We got a fighter coming in!" And suddenly—boom—boots thundered down the stairs like a herd of caffeinated buffalo. Male deputies piled over each other, tripping, elbowing, practically frothing at the mouth just to be first on the scene. All trying to get a piece of the action, like it was Black Friday at Walmart, and someone just restocked the flat screens.

To me, the whole spectacle was mildly horrifying—grown men competing for the chance to wrestle a drunk guy in cargo shorts. But worse than the enthusiasm was the instigation. Every now and then, one of them would quietly crank a wristlock just past the point of "compliance," as they called it, and straight into "let's-start-a-fight-for-fun" territory.

Chapter Four: Playing with the Boys

It wasn't official policy, of course. Just a little extracurricular creativity.

I stood back and took notes—mental ones, mostly. Like: *Don't start fights. Don't cheer for fights. And definitely don't lose a shoe while charging downstairs to join one.*

This wasn't the only thing about jail that collided head-on with whatever fragile scraps of Christianity and morality I'd managed to cling to. No, there were plenty more moral speed bumps ahead.

Take intake for female arrestees, for instance. Once it was clear a woman wasn't getting the quick "book and release" deal, she had to be housed—and that meant the strip-down show. A female deputy would lead her into a "private" cell (privacy here is a relative term, mostly meaning no male deputies watching) and deliver the official announcement: it was time to disrobe.

Every orifice, crack, and crevice had to be exposed and inspected. No weapons, no drugs, no surprises. The logic was sound—security first, dignity somewhere much farther down the list. The deputy circled, eyes sharp for anything out of place, like a hawk hunting for contraband.

Once "cleared," the arrestee could finally slip into the glorified prison couture: the standard-issue orange jumpsuit, the unofficial uniform of humility.

In my head, I knew this was a practical necessity—not a punishment or deliberate humiliation. But in reality? It *was* humiliating. Strip-searched and scrutinized like a sandwich at airport security. Morality, dignity, and compassion all got quietly shoved aside for the sake of control and safety.

One night, a woman was led through the intake ritual—the strip-down, the inspection, the final swap into the jail's signature jumpsuit. She moved with a calm that caught me off guard, like she was stepping onto a stage she'd rehearsed a thousand times before.

Her eyes didn't dart around or plead for mercy. Instead, they held a quiet steadiness, the kind that says, *You can take my clothes, my freedom, even my dignity—but you can't touch what's inside.*

She peeled off her jacket, then her shirt, each movement deliberate, measured—not defiant, but unbroken. When the deputy started the inspection, she stood still, almost regal, like a statue carved from years of hard lessons and silent endurance.

There was no bitterness, no self-pity, just a steady breath and an unspoken refusal to be diminished. I watched and felt something shift—a grudging respect for a kind of strength that doesn't roar or fight, but simply *is*.

In that sterile, fluorescent-lit cell, where vulnerability was forced and dignity stripped away, she was a quiet rebellion.

Seeing human beings on both sides of the bars was surprisingly illuminating, inmates and Jail Deputies. It made me reach for Viktor Frankl's *Man's Search for Meaning*, that 1946 classic where Frankl recounts his time as a prisoner of war and distills life's purpose into three paths: completing meaningful tasks, caring for others, and finding meaning by facing suffering with dignity.

Most inmates seemed to cling to that third path—the quiet, often invisible struggle to find purpose and dignity amid hardship. Meanwhile, many deputies did not seem to have deep introspection, they seemed to stop at the first two paths; finishing the shift

Chapter Four: Playing with the Boys

and maybe, just maybe, look out for a fellow human when they could.

For the inmates booked and housed overnight, a Bible waited quietly in each cell—like a small, worn lifeline tucked into the corner. Some knew exactly why it was there, clutching its pages with gratitude, seeking comfort or guidance in God's words when everything else felt lost.

Others, though, treated it like a foreign artifact—never cracked open, maybe never even touched. Much to my surprise, that included some deputies, too, Leonard among them. He'd scoff quietly, saying, "Don't need no book to know how messed up this place is."

The Bible sat there, a silent witness to faith, skepticism, hope, and everything in between.

One night, feeling particularly evangelical, I asked Leonard if he'd seen *The Passion of the Christ*—it was playing at the theater then. He'd seen it, alright, but couldn't make heads or tails of it. "Why would anyone sit through two hours of some guy getting beaten, whipped, humiliated, and then crucified?" he asked, genuinely baffled.

My brain scrambled to find a place to start explaining a story so vast and complex it deserved more than five minutes and a snack break. "How much world history do you know?" I asked.

"None," he said flatly.

So, night after night, the small classroom of our jail cell became our chapel. We read, talked, argued, and learned. Piece by piece, the story unfolded—a strange, heavy grace shared in whispers under fluorescent lights and the low hum of the night shift.

I began carefully. "Christianity introduced a new idea: one God who loves His people—unlike the old Pagan gods, who were many, selfish, and never satisfied." Leonard listened, eyebrows furrowed but curious.

"Jesus, the Son of God, was seen as a threat—a revolutionary to the Pharisees and Sadducees. They didn't like His message: that everyone would be judged equally, and their fate—Heaven or Hell—depended on how they lived here on earth."

I paused, then added, "One of Christ's most famous teachings is the Beatitudes. You might've heard this one: 'Blessed are they who hunger and thirst for righteousness, for they shall be filled.' It's about longing for something better, something pure—and being promised it in return."

Leonard nodded slowly, the wheels turning.

I felt scattered, like a radio tuning in and out, struggling to find a clear place to begin. But I kept going. Leonard seemed to enjoy the "classes," whether because they made the nights pass faster or because he genuinely found something in the lessons. Either way, he kept showing up.

And somewhere in that cramped, fluorescent-lit jail, I found a part of myself I hadn't quite met before: teacher. Who would've thought?

A quiet hope took root—a little voice nudging me, *Someday, you'll finish college. For real this time.*

Many inmates buried themselves in books to kill time, emerging surprisingly well-versed in law, philosophy, math, and science. Some were grinding through their GEDs, others chasing college degrees behind bars.

Chapter Four: Playing with the Boys

There were a few I looked forward to visiting—conversations that sparked unexpectedly in the fluorescent haze, ranging from Socrates to quadratic equations.

Then, just as the discussion hit a stride, chaos would break loose—a deputy barreling down the hall, black marker in hand, wild-eyed and grinning like a kid on a sugar high, swiping at another deputy's uniform. They'd crash into desks, bump into each other, the whole circus stampeding past.

The inmates, ever the wise observers, would watch with quiet, knowing looks—some barely concealing their disbelief that their so-called guards could behave like playground bullies.

It was annoying. It was childish. And honestly, I felt sorry for the inmates—they had more maturity than the people supposed to keep order.

Friday nights earned the nickname "Dog Pile Night." Far from the smooth, professional handling I'd imagined, these takedowns usually looked like a wrestling match gone off the rails—arms and legs flailing, hats flying, deputies piling on like a pack of wild dogs trying to subdue a squirrel.

To my eye, it was complete overkill. But the unspoken rule was clear: jump in and help, or risk becoming the deputy everyone whispered about in the break room.

That logic never sat right with me. For someone obsessed with precision and understanding, there had to be a better way.

So, off I went—found a local martial arts studio and signed up for Jujitsu. Because if you're going to dive into a pile of chaos, you might as well learn how to do it with style.

On my first day, Chantelle approached with an easy smile. She wore a thick cotton jacket wrapped tightly around her chest, layered over a simple t-shirt and cinched with a sturdy brown belt. Her pants were the same—baggy, white, and tough as old canvas. Later, I learned the whole outfit, called a gi, was designed so you could grab hold and throw the heck out of someone without tearing your clothes.

"Hi, I'm Chantelle. Welcome aboard!" she said, her grin infectious.

Introducing myself to her, I said, "Honestly, I'm here because I want to learn how to put on a proper wrist lock."

Chantelle laughed. "Oh, you'll learn that—and so much more. Plus, it's a lot of fun."

She was right. Those classes felt like pure bliss. Maybe it was the wrestling with my brothers all those years ago that made it come naturally. Or maybe it was something deeper—the chance to step outside the roles I'd worn for so long: not just part of a big family, not just Lorenzo's wife or the kids' mom, but someone carving out her own space.

Wrist locks are a cornerstone of Jiu Jitsu—and deceptively powerful. Even a fully armored Samurai wouldn't find much comfort in them. Armor might stop a sword, but it's no match for a joint manipulated just right.

The beauty of a wrist lock lies in its subtle brutality: it takes away an opponent's primary weapon—their hands—without throwing a single punch. Suddenly, their whole arsenal becomes useless.

Chapter Four: Playing with the Boys

These moves serve as solid defenses, effective restraints, and occasionally, a rather pointed reminder of who's in control. The pain isn't just unpleasant—it's the kind that leaves no doubt you've lost the argument.

The first time I tried a wrist lock on a sparring partner, I figured it would be like gently guiding a reluctant dog on a leash. Instead, it felt like I'd accidentally tuned into a Masterclass on how quickly someone can regret underestimating you.

I grabbed his wrist, twisted just so, and immediately saw his face change—confusion, then surprise, then full-on "oh no" panic. His body stiffened, a low curse slipped out, and he started bargaining for mercy like he was haggling at a flea market.

"Okay, okay! You got me!" he gasped, half laughing, half wheezing.

In that moment, I understood why wrist locks are such a favorite: a small move with a disproportionate impact. It's like the ultimate mic drop in a fight—quiet, precise, and devastating.

Six years passed, and with them came a deep, firsthand education in what "pain compliance" truly meant. It wasn't just about hurting someone—it was about control, balance, and knowing exactly where to apply pressure without losing yourself.

I learned to center—not just physically but mentally. To quiet the chaos inside and find a calm focus that let me steer both mind and body like a well-tuned machine. It wasn't a skill you picked up and shelved. No, this was a lifetime's work, a relentless dance of practice and patience.

And somewhere along the way, I picked up a new companion for the journey: *The Book of Five Rings*. A manual not just of swordsmanship but strategy, discipline, and understanding conflict in ways that went far beyond the dojo.

1. Think of what is right and true.
2. Practice and cultivate the science.
3. Become acquainted with the arts.
4. Know the principles of crafts.
5. Understand the harm and benefit in everything.
6. Learn to see everything accurately.
7. Become aware of what is not obvious.
8. Be careful even in small matters. Do not do anything useless.

Truths. That's what *The Book of Five Rings* delivered in spades. It wasn't the kind of book you simply read and shelve. No—you read a passage, then set it down, eyes distant, turning its ideas over and over like a puzzle in your mind. So many concepts seemed to reach right into your own life, answering questions you'd carried around, unspoken and unresolved.

And then, suddenly, a sentence would strike you—full force, right in the chest. It was your sentence. The one you couldn't ignore.

For me, that sentence was about Lorenzo, both angry at him and sad for him.

"It's a confounding thing when one person sees their wrongs and is humble enough to change for the better and yet another refuses to see and will not change."

Chapter Four: Playing with the Boys

That line hit home—not in a dramatic, life-altering way, but in that quiet, uncomfortable *"yep, that's us"* sort of way. It reminded me of what I'd been brushing under the rug for years.

Lorenzo was still drinking, and I was still avoiding the conversation. I kept myself busy with the kids, shuttling them to soccer fields, piano recitals, and orthodontist appointments, while he stayed stuck in a cycle of discontent. He always seemed distant, weighed down by things he couldn't—or wouldn't—talk about. We all tried, in our own ways, to bring him back into the fold, to get him to laugh, to participate. But it rarely worked. His silence filled the house more than any argument ever could.

And still, I carried on, telling myself it wasn't that bad. Because sometimes, telling yourself that is easier than asking what happens if it *is*.

Chapter Five

Jewels in Heaven

Johnny Cash crackled through the Eight-Track, the kind of sound that felt like it had gravel in its throat. We cruised down the highway at a steady pace, the *whoosh-whoosh-whoosh* of the trees flying past syncing perfectly with the rhythm of the song. For a moment, it felt like I *was* on that train he was singing about.

"*I hear that train a'comin', it's comin' 'round the bend...*" Dad belted out right on cue, grinning like a kid in a candy store. "*And I ain't seen the sunshine since I don't know when...*" He was in his element—hands on the wheel, wind in his hair, a big rig under him, and all of us packed in behind. You'd have thought he was leading a parade instead of hauling a busload of kids.

Mom, ever the daredevil, would make her way down the narrow aisle like a circus performer—mug of hot coffee in hand, timing her steps with the bumps in the road. Somehow, miraculously, she never spilled a drop. When she finally reached the front, she'd slide in behind Dad and start rubbing his shoulders like a co-pilot on a long-haul mission.

"Look, kids!" Mom would chirp from the front, channeling her inner tour guide, determined to educate, inform, and—if we were lucky—entertain at least one of us. "That sign says *The Eisenhower Interstate System!* Did you know he was the president responsible for building America's highway system?"

Chapter Five: Jewels in Heaven

We barely had time to nod before she was off again, undeterred by our glazed expressions.

"He was also a five-star General who helped win World War II—and get this—*both* political parties wanted him to run for president. Imagine that! Isn't that interesting?"

We'd all grunt in semi-agreement, unsure whether we were more impressed by Eisenhower or by Mom's ability to deliver a full-on PBS special from the front seat of a moving vehicle.

Sometimes, it was hard to tell where Mom's facts ended, and her fiction began. "Look at that sign, kids," she'd announce, pointing out the window. "It says *Falling Rock*. Did you know there was once a Native American chief who lost his son in a great buffalo stampede? His name was Falling Rock. He searched far and wide for his boy, and to this very day, you'll see signs across the country where he continued the search."

We all nodded solemnly, as if a missing child bulletin really could be posted on a highway slope.

It was a good story—sweet, even. But I started doing the math in my head. Where exactly did Chief Falling Rock get metal signs and reflective paint? Did he also have a DOT permit?

That's how you know you're getting older: you stop enjoying the silly just for the sake of silly. And maybe that's the saddest part of growing up—not the losing of innocence, but the gaining of logic.

Mile after mile, we found ways to keep ourselves entertained, some more effective than others. There was playing endless rounds of *"I spy with my little eye,"* repeated so many times it practically became a chant, and then there was Paul and his guitar.

Paul strummed away like he was auditioning for a cross-country tour no one asked for, until Mom, somewhere around mile marker 200, would inevitably snap: "For God's sake, Paul—*please stop!*"

No matter where we went—desert, mountains, middle-of-nowhere—Mom had this uncanny ability to sniff out a Catholic church like a bloodhound on a holy mission. It didn't matter the city or how obscure the neighborhood—somehow, she'd find one. Little chapels tucked behind gas stations, grand cathedrals with golden domes—God always answered her internal mapping system.

It honestly felt like she had some kind of divine walkie-talkie. She'd ask, and God would just... answer.

Apparently, that gift skipped most of us and landed squarely on Vincent. That kid loved church. While the rest of us dragged our heels like we were being led into Sunday detention, he practically skipped up the steps.

Starting in second grade, he'd march right up to a priest—total stranger—and ask if they needed an altar server. Most of the time, they did. He'd stay after Mass, wiping down chalices and clearing the altar, while the rest of us sat on the bus, tapping our feet and eyeing the nearest drive-thru.

Mom would smile at our impatience and say, *"Just be patient. He's earning his jewels in Heaven."*

Some people are born with a clear channel to the Lord. My brother? Five bars and full signal.

Chapter Five: Jewels in Heaven

Me? I had questions. Like Confession. Did defending myself count as a sin? Because if it did, I definitely had some explaining to do.

"Forgive me, Father, for I have sinned. I threw wet manure at my brother… but it was in self-defense. Yes, I could've picked up some dry stuff, Father, but time was of the essence. He was gaining on me, and the wet pile was right there—it was a tactical decision."

Confession always left me slightly confused. The line between sin and survival felt pretty blurry when you grew up in a pack of siblings with the reflexes of wild animals. But despite the theological gray areas, I secretly enjoyed going to church—maybe not the kneeling or the fire-and-brimstone talk, but the *people*, the *music*, and the *potlucks*.

Catholic churches were big on potlucks. No matter the town, the state, or the liturgical season, there was bound to be a long folding table covered in casseroles, deviled eggs, and enough Jell-O to fuel a small army. In a large family, that was gold. At potlucks, seconds weren't a luxury—they were a strategy. You just had to move fast and make peace with the mystery meat.

The day we got kicked out of church started the night before, in Napa Valley. Dad had parked the bus at the campground, and since the night was unusually warm, he left the doors wide open. That's when Heidi made her move—creeping out into the dark on a little midnight hunt.

In our chaotic family, dogs tend to pick their favorite human, and Heidi's allegiance was clear: Dad. Among all the noisy kids and constant chaos, he was her steady rock, the one who gave her a sense of order and calm. Their bond was something you couldn't break.

To prove her loyalty, Heidi had a habit of bringing home trophies from her hunts—usually harmless gophers, a kind of canine calling card. But this time, she outdid herself. Instead of a gopher, she proudly dropped a skunk carcass right at the foot of the bus stairs.

Around five in the morning, the unmistakable stench started creeping throughout the bus and into our noses, dragging all ten of us out of sleep. Like a bat signal for disaster, we made a beeline for the front door and bottlenecked there. Marc, who got fed up with waiting, slipped out the emergency back door like a ninja in slippers.

As we poured out, gasping for fresh air, all ten of us took turns berating Heidi—the poor dog looked utterly bewildered. Dad, however, dragged her off, tied her to a tree, and set out to buy gallons of tomato juice—the legendary cure-all for skunk smell.

Sunday morning church was still non-negotiable. Mom was adamant we show up, smelling like a skunk or not. Elizabeth, the oldest at sixteen, protested loudly,

" No, Mom, We *stink*!"

"Now, kids," she said with all the wisdom of a seasoned mom, "there's a lesson here. When life gives you lemons, you make lemonade. The smell's not that bad. The skunk didn't even get inside the bus, and none of us touched it."

And just like that, the argument was over. We lined up, still grimacing, while Mom sprayed us down with her trusty can of Ly-

Chapter Five: Jewels in Heaven

sol—her go-to miracle cure for everything from odors to bad moods.

We took up an entire pew as usual—no small feat with our crew—and Mass began. Just as the priest launched into his sermon about collecting your jewels in Heaven, not here on Earth, I heard Marc lean over to Dad and whisper, "Dad, there's nobody sitting in the pews next to us."

Dad kept his head bowed, hands tightly clasped, but his eyes darted upward, scanning the sanctuary. Quietly, he whispered back, "Holy cow... you're right."

Apparently, the entire congregation had given us a wide berth—as if we were a walking biohazard. Mom, eyes closed and head tilted reverently toward heaven, was blissfully unaware... until Dad tapped her shoulder. She opened her eyes, glanced around, and her mouth dropped open in horror. Their eyes both locked on the priest, who was staring right back at them with a look that could curdle milk.

When the congregation finally stood, the ushers wasted no time. Like a reluctant herd, they began shepherding us out the door.

The Napa Valley of my youth wasn't about wine—it was about the Mediterranean warmth in the air, the rugged Mayacamas Mountains standing guard to the west, and the Vaca Mountains rising to the east. Calistoga, resting at the foot of Mount Saint Helena, felt tucked away in a quiet valley about 360 feet above sea level. Grasses swayed in the breeze, winding creeks carved their way through the land, and giant twisted oaks draped in soft, lacy moss filled the air with the fresh, earthy scent of damp wood and pine needles.

Lake Berryessa, the largest lake in Napa County, was the shining centerpiece. My parents had a lifetime membership at the Napa Valley Ranch Club, and the gatekeeper knew our bus well—no need to check permits, just a friendly wave to let us in.

The campground felt like a small sanctuary for campers: paved bike paths, a cool pool, a quiet library, an arcade with the faint smell of popcorn, and, best of all, a creek that threaded through the whole park. Its banks were lined with soft grass, and tall oaks and aspens cast dappled shadows that danced in the sunlight. The creek itself was alive—buzzing with minnows darting beneath the surface and crawdads scuttling over the rocks.

Occasionally, Grandma would join us, usually parked in a lawn chair right next to Mom. Most days, you'd find them deep in their own little world with the paper, Grandma chatting away, like two wrens locked on the same juicy worm. Nothing, not even the world ending could pull them away once they'd locked in.

Of course, I picked exactly that moment to speak up. "Mom," I said, trying to sound patient but clearly losing steam after waiting for what felt like an eternity, "I've been waiting here patiently for about an hour, and I'd like to ask you something."

They both looked up at me like I'd just snatched their worm right out from under their beaks. Mom craned her neck, eyebrows furrowed, eyes narrowing in disbelief. "Wha??"

"Can I have a horse?"

"No! Now go play."

Chapter Five: Jewels in Heaven

Chased away and dismissed again, I grabbed my pile of plastic farm animals and horses and trudged outside to pout in the sandbox. Not long after, Blaise plopped down beside me with a grin and asked, "You wanna play army?"

Oh, boy. I've danced this dance before. My mind immediately flashed to all the times "playing army" meant chaos and wrestling matches disguised as games. Blaise, however, was on a charm offensive.

"I'll be nice this time, I swear."

I squinted at him skeptically. "I don't see how army guys are gonna play with farm animals."

"Trust me," he said with way too much confidence, "I'll play nice."

Trying to give him the benefit of the doubt, and probably setting myself up for trouble, I finally relented.

Blaise was an incredible little architect, fences crafted from twigs and string, tiny huts with thatched roofs meticulously stitched together using a sewing needle and dried grass. He carved out winding roads and even planted miniature fake trees to decorate their tiny village. Sitting in the warm sand, heated by the sun, I felt a rare peace, proud of the small world we'd built together.

Then, without warning, the calm shattered. Blaise unleashed his battle cry, his screech echoing like an F-14 Tomcat fighter jet roaring overhead. "Bamp ccrrrrr, crash pluuu…" spittle flying from his mouth as he enthusiastically bombed the village to oblivion.

He grabbed one of my cows, grinned wickedly, and declared, "Sorry, Mame, but my men need to eat," before pretending to slice it open with a plastic knife. That was it. I gathered up the few animals that survived the attack and made a beeline for the bus—right past Mom and Grandma, who didn't so much as pause their conversation or glance my way.

During the long summer months, Dad would park the bus at the Ranch, grab his company truck, and head off to work for the week, leaving us behind to enjoy the quiet. All summer long, we watched the steady flow of visitors—Friday nights, the parking lot would fill up like clockwork, and by Sunday morning, it would empty out again, leaving the place all to ourselves.

This time, though, our stay was short—just two days—because Monday morning brought appointments no one could miss. But Monday didn't start on time. Dad was going to be late for work and needed to find a pay phone to call and let his bosses know.

Our job—look for a phone booth! Lined up like sentinels—four kids pressed against each window on one side of the bus, four on the other—each desperately scanning the horizon for that elusive glass box.

"There! There's one, Dad!" Vince beamed, pointing excitedly at a grocery store parking lot.

The bus slowed, then spun on a dime, hopping the curb as we all lurched skyward—pots and pans rattling like a runaway percussion band. It finally came to a stop, perfectly straddling three parking spaces like it was claiming territory.

Dad jumped out and jogged to the phone booth to call work. Meanwhile, because someone was always hungry, Mom pulled out her frying pan and started fixing something for someone to eat.

Chapter Five: Jewels in Heaven

Like clockwork, she dumped that pan onto the stove, lit the propane, and began frying up a tortilla with some cheese.

Some days, it wasn't tortillas—it was a watermelon. The big, unwieldy thing always lived in the sink because it was too large for any cupboard. If not secured there, it would roll wild and free across the bus, forcing us into a chaotic chase.

Down the aisle it would roll, followed by Mom's unmistakable cry, "Go get the watermelon!"

"I got it last time!"

"Oh, for heaven's sakes, Becca—just go get the watermelon."

One day, we heard the low rumble of another engine pulling in next to us. Another converted bus rolled up beside us and parked with the practiced ease of a fellow road veteran.

Then—clear as a bell and twice as theatrical—a voice rang out across our bow: "Ahoy there, in the bus!"

It felt less like a parking lot and more like a harbor suddenly, two ships meeting mid-journey, their captains calling through the fog.

A man, maybe in his late thirties and wearing the road like a second skin, ambled over to Dad, who was crouched beside the bus working on something mechanical-looking and mysterious. Encounters like this were common. On our travels, we often came across all kinds of conversions—camper vans, patched-up station wagons, homemade trailers, even old school buses like ours. There was always a quiet recognition between travelers, a kind of nod that said, *you get it.*

Introductions were casual and sincere, usually followed by an open invitation to "come aboard" and check out each other's handiwork. Once inside, the conversation shifted easily to battle stories of life on the road: propane leaks, leaky water lines, electrical ghosts, and the ever-elusive alternator failure. "Not enough RPMs to handle the weight," someone would say, or "Fuel line was so clogged I thought I'd blown the whole engine."

These weren't complaints, they were badges of honor. Folks shared what they'd learned, what they'd rigged, what had miraculously held together. And every now and then, someone would share how they'd been politely nudged out of a campground for not having one of those sparkling rigs with slide-outs and satellite dishes.

But among the roll-yer-own crowd, none of that mattered. You had a story, a roof that mostly held, and four tires with dreams. That was enough.

The man introduced himself as Troy, scratching the back of his neck like he was already half-apologizing for the favor he was about to ask. He wondered if Dad might take a look at a few mechanical problems on his bus. As they talked, the door behind him creaked open and out stepped his wife, followed by a little girl about my age, both of them squinting in the sunlight and easing in close behind him like backup singers waiting for their cue.

Dad was usually the first to offer help—and in this case, he didn't even wait for the full story. But even before the formal invitation was made, I had noticed their bus was... different. Any kid could've told you that. For starters, it looked like someone had painted it with leftover buckets from a dozen garage sales—splashes of teal, orange, green, and something that might have once

Chapter Five: Jewels in Heaven

been pink. The windows weren't just dirty; some were cracked, others patched with duct tape and dreams.

Still, Troy was vibrating with curiosity, his eyes darting around our rig like he couldn't wait to see how we'd pulled it off. So, Dad, proud as ever, welcomed them aboard. He walked Troy through every detail—the propane line that fed the stove and water heater, the web of electrical switches, the exhaust fan he'd installed in the bathroom with surgical precision. He pointed out the bunks, explaining how they were both braced and beautiful, sturdy enough to survive a mountain road but nice enough not to look like prison cots.

Troy didn't say much. He rubbed his chin, nodded here and there, and soaked it all in like someone studying for a test he hadn't known was coming.

Then it was our turn to see the inside of their bus, and they invited us in.

As we climbed the steps into their bus, it became clear that the confusion of colors outside wasn't just skin deep—it had spilled inside, too. The original seats were gone, replaced by what felt more like the inside of a large camping tent than a home. A folding card table stood off-kilter near the front. A hibachi grill sat right on the floor, like a fire hazard waiting to happen. An ice chest doubled as a refrigerator. It was less of a conversion and more of a collection—of ideas, of effort, of stuff that might work *for now*.

Troy, eager for approval, kept glancing at Dad as he led us through. "Andy, what do you think of what I've done here?" he asked brightly, grabbing a bare lightbulb dangling from a loose wire. The wire looped through a hook screwed into the bus's ceiling, then disappeared somewhere into the wall like a trail of hope.

Dad didn't answer right away. He squinted slightly, as if suddenly aware of a sunflower seed wedged in his back molar, working at it with his tongue while buying time. "Um," he finally said. "Good work, Troy."

But I could see it—Dad's inner mechanic was weeping. Troy didn't "get it." He had heart, no doubt, but not the wiring plan to match.

Still, as Troy continued the grand tour, pointing proudly at every makeshift fix and feature, Dad kept smiling, nodding along with quiet encouragement.

"That's great, Troy," he said with a warmth that said *I admire your spirit, if not your circuitry.*

As I trailed behind during the grand tour of their bus, something started to nag at me. We'd seen the card table, the grill, even a pile of mismatched pillows—but no sign of a bathroom.

I cleared my throat and asked as plainly as I could, "Um... where do you go to the bathroom?"

Without missing a beat, the little girl darted behind a box and came back grinning, hoisting up a battered red Folgers coffee can like it was a trophy.

"Right here! This is my Pee-Pee can!"

She was so proud. I was... less so.

Dad's eyes flicked to the window just in time to spot Mom walking across the parking lot with two bags of groceries. That was his cue.

Chapter Five: Jewels in Heaven

"Uh, well—looks like we gotta get going," he said quickly, clapping his hands once like a coach ending practice.

We hustled out of there—down their steps, up ours, and pulled out of that parking lot faster than you could say my grandma's favorite cuss word: *Sugar Molasses.*

"Sit down, everyone!" Dad barked, shifting into gear.

"But, Andy," Mom protested, arms still full of groceries, "I haven't even put the food away!"

Dad didn't answer. He just kept driving.

"It's okay, we gotta get going," Dad muttered, eyes fixed on the road.

"But Andy," Mom pressed, arms still full of groceries, "it seemed like those folks really needed your help. You know what Father said about storing up treasures in heaven, not here on earth. It's our acts of kindness, our help to others, that get us to heaven—not the things we hoard."

Dad's jaw tightened. Then, without missing a beat, he shot back, "It'll be a cold day in hell before I help that stupid SOB."

Mom didn't say another word. Dad slammed the gas, careening over the parking lot curb. The bus jolted, then bounced like a rubber ball on a driveway.

That night I wrote in my journal: *Things aren't always what they seem. And collecting your jewels in heaven? Sometimes, that's the hardest act of all.*

———————— ✤ ————————

Working the graveyard shift, I found the jail starts to quiet down around 1:00 a.m. Aside from the occasional shout echoing between cells, the soundscape softens—snoring inmates fill the silence, and the steady tapping of typewriters accompanies deputies as they finish their daily logs. When there's nothing left to do, many of us pass the time with a book. Flannery O'Connor's *A Good Man is Hard to Find* seemed like a good one given where I was working. A family sets off on vacation with a grandmother who's self-absorbed and more than a little sharp-tongued. She steers the trip into trouble, unwittingly leading them straight into the path of an escaped convict on a lonely country road. One by one, the family members are taken away—and murdered—until only the grandmother remains.

> *"...the misfit sprang back as if a snake had bitten him and shot her three times through the chest. Then he put his gun down on the ground and took off his glasses and began to clean them. Hiram and Bobby Lee returned from the woods and stood over the ditch, looking down at the grandmother who half sat and half lay in a puddle of blood with her legs crossed under her like a child's and her face smiling up at the cloudless sky. ....take her off and throw her where you thrown the others." He said....."*

O'Connor's stories read like modern Greek tragedies—her female protagonists often start out as arrogant know-it-alls, only to face a brutal reckoning that forces them to confront their own flaws, usually far too late. Flannery was a brilliant writer and psy-

Chapter Five: Jewels in Heaven

chologist. She doesn't ask readers to simply lament the existence of demons in the world; instead, she urges us to acknowledge that they are real—and to see the world as it truly is, not as we wish it to be.

After seven years working in the jail, I got a surprise: I was selected to move up to patrol. It felt like winning the lottery, if the prize was six months of sweat, shouting, and shin splints. The police academy loomed ahead like a boot-camp buffet, but I didn't care. Just the thought of leaving the jail behind made me feel like I was being O.R.'d—released on my own recognizance, no bail required. And trust me, after seven years in lockup, even if you're the one with the keys—that's a miracle.

There were fifty of us—forty-five men and five women—crammed into the same nervous, hopeful group.

On the very first day, everyone yelled at us. I stood as straight, plain, and tall as I could, hoping not to draw any extra attention.

The Drill Sergeant planted himself in front of the guy next to me and barked, "What the hell is that on your face? Two days' worth of facial hair? Didn't you bother to shave?"

The Drill Sergeant was short, red-faced, and reminded me of the Chicken Hawk from some Looney Tunes cartoon I'd seen as a kid. A laugh bubbled up inside me, threatening to escape. But I clamped my mouth shut and made a promise: no yelling at me on this first day.

The police academy isn't the military. There is a big difference there. In the military, quitting isn't an option; you're in it for better or worse. But at the police academy? You can quit anytime, or more likely, they'll find some tiny mistake to kick you out. And believe me, they become experts at spotting every missed step or misplaced comma like hawks hunting for prey.

Each academy prides itself on forging top-notch officers, highlighting their policy of cutting 5 to 10 percent of every class. The catch? Sometimes, it feels like those cuts come down to a lottery more than anything else. You watch promising recruits—sharp, eager, ready to serve—shown the door, while a few of the less-than-stellar characters slip through the cracks with a polite smile and a "good luck."

It's like trying to pick the ripest apples from a barrel while blindfolded—some fall to the floor, and some bruised ones make it into the basket.

After living and working for the Air Force, I've found that although the police academy attempts to emulate the military academy, they are different. Yes, there is a drill sergeant and inspections and uniforms, but there are stark differences, the biggest, most of us were older. Way beyond the average age of a military enlistee, which is around eighteen. Another difference, in the military the recruits volunteer for misery. They'll hike through deserts in gear that looks like it was rejected by a WWII surplus bin, and eat food that tastes like bugs.

The police academy, though? Whole different animal. You can't show up with broken gear or skip meals to prove how tough you are. Do that, and you'll "wash out"—which is a polite way of saying "fired, with sweat stains and debt." And the stress? Oh, it's there. But it's not from a drill-sergeant barking in your face—though we had a few who tried. The real stress came from the inside: tuition bills, crabby toddlers, a mortgage, a spouse who wants

Chapter Five: Jewels in Heaven

to know why you thought becoming a cop at thirty-eight was a good idea. Marines get screamed at to build mental toughness. Police recruits are annoyed by it.

But I was ready. I *knew* I was ready. Because when you grow up with six brothers—and one of them is named *Blaise*—you've already survived a daily boot camp. You don't flinch at yelling. You flinch when you hear, "Blaise has your diary." That's real fear.

The first week was a blur of gear, government-issued binders, and panic. We were herded into orientation, handed what felt like fifty books—Penal Code, procedure manuals, rules, rules about rules. Then came the uniform parade: PT sweats, cadet gear, shirts, pants, lockers, and lists of what we'd need to survive the next six months.

The academy compound would quickly become our second home, and like any home, there were rooms you loved—and rooms you'd rather set on fire. The gym? Oh, we *knew* the gym. That's where we got lovingly broken during physical training, flung around in weaponless defense class, and staged high-drama shootouts with rubber guns and bruised egos.

Then there was the driving simulator room, with giant wraparound screens that looked like a video game, only with more paperwork and fewer lives. We practiced everything from high-speed chases to parallel parking under pressure. Spoiler: the cone never made it.

And the classroom. *That* classroom. We lived in that thing. Report writing, legal lectures, tests, more lectures, and enough caffeine to fuel a small city. Every time we escaped for a day at the shooting range or the driving course, it felt like recess for grown-ups—with firearms and squad cars. But by the end of that first week, I missed my kids—bad. And I wasn't alone. You could feel it in the air: a quiet ache under the uniforms and bravado. Come Friday afternoon, no one lingered. As soon as we were dismissed, the parking lot emptied like someone had pulled a fire alarm. Engines revved, doors slammed, and just like that, we were gone—each of us barreling down the highway toward something soft, familiar, and preferably not shouting drill commands.

Our days were jam-packed: morning lectures, lunchtime mysteries from the cafeteria, midafternoon workouts designed by sadists, then back to the classroom for more death by PowerPoint. The firing range? Two to three days a week—more if we missed the target and hit the dirt.

Some tests were pass-and-move-on. Others? Pass or pack it up and leave the campus for good. The Wall was one of those. Six feet of psychological warfare. Most folks could muscle over it with a little technique and determination. But if your brain said "nope," your body followed. Fast.

Then there was Range. You fail the shooting test, you're out. Because let's be honest—no one wants a cop who can't hit the broad side of a donut shop.

As the weeks wore on, the stiff cadet facades began to crack. Personalities—once buttoned up tighter than our uniform collars—started to surface. Some cadets walked around like they had something to prove, chests puffed out, eyes scanning for invisible doubters. They didn't just want the badge—they needed it to become someone.

Chapter Five: Jewels in Heaven

Others were less loud, but just as telling. Oneta, for example, came from the jail. She missed her logbooks, her inmates, and her chair—especially the chair. At the academy, there were no Frappuccinos, no routine, and definitely no place to sit. She wore defeat like it was part of the uniform. You could tell: this was not her battlefield.

Then there was Mike. Quiet, steady, always thinking. He had that calm, natural authority—like if there was a fire, you'd just look at him and wait for orders. He laughed sometimes, but it always felt like he was enjoying some private, philosophical angle on the joke. Getting to know him was like untying a knot underwater—possible, but slow.

Dave had been an elementary school teacher but bailed for better pay. With a wife and three kids to support, he said finger paints and fractions weren't cutting it. He wasn't the only career jumper—our group included a florist, a horseshoer, and a surveyor. Their stories made me uneasy. Maybe the grass isn't greener—maybe we're all just sprinting from one patch of dying turf to another, hoping this one feels right underfoot. I had always thought finishing college would fix that hollow ache in my chest. But now I wasn't so sure. Yes, I was intellectually restless. Yes, I was married to an alcoholic. But was I chasing a calling—or just hopping life rafts before one sank completely? Hard to say. Either way, I was in now. The uniform fit, the clock was ticking, and self-reflection would have to wait until after firearms training.

The academy had a way of bending your sense of logic and fairness until it snapped. Eventually, we all just shrugged and muttered the unofficial motto: *Play the game.*

One day during firearms training, Dave—our soft-spoken former schoolteacher—was reminded for the hundredth time to be more assertive. The scenario began: Dave crouched behind his patrol car's engine block, fake gun in hand, ready for action.

Then the instructor barked a command—muffled, vague, unintelligible. Nobody heard it, least of all Dave. So, he did what they kept telling him to do: he spoke up.

"WHAT DID YOU SAY? WHAT DID YOU SAY?"

Apparently, this was the wrong kind of assertive. The instructor's face twisted.

"Are you yelling at me? *Are you yelling at me?* Get off the scenario. Sit this one out!"

The room went still. His voice was harsh, clipped, and completely over the top. I sat there blinking, trying to decode what lesson was supposedly hidden in that outburst. Maybe there wasn't one. Maybe it wasn't about training at all—just a man on a power trip, teaching us the real rules of the game: don't embarrass the instructor, and never, ever yell *back? I had no idea what to make of this.*

About a week later, we were all sitting in the classroom, waiting for the next joy to begin, when the Drill Sergeant burst through the door, holding up a crumpled silver gum wrapper like it was the Crown Jewels.

"You see this gum wrapper?" he thundered. "A gum wrapper *just like this* was spotted on the parking lot. Cadet Jones—*Cadet Jones!* —was seen picking it up. I and another instructor watched him walk over and *dispose* of it properly."

He paused for effect, eyes blazing.

Chapter Five: Jewels in Heaven

"This—*this*—is the kind of selfless attention to detail and pride that makes an upstanding cadet! It's behavior *we want to see from all of you!*"

A gum wrapper. The academy had officially lost its mind. But honestly? I kind of wanted to stand up and salute. Because if saving the world started with picking up trash, maybe we had a chance after all.

Was he for real? *That* was exemplary behavior in the Police Academy? I hope the gum bandit never crosses paths with that cop—he'd be booked for littering and community service before you can say "citizen's arrest."

Trying to keep fifty grown cadets from bursting into laughter? That's a monumental achievement all on its own. The lump in your throat burns, your cheeks twitch, and when you glance sideways to see a whole row of cadets convulsing in suppressed giggles—*now* that's what I call exemplary.

Week one at the range, we lost our first recruit: Cliff. He was a gun enthusiast's dream—always talking "gun this, gun that," waving his hands around like a conductor... except one hand was holding a loaded pistol. The Range Masters didn't appreciate the showmanship. One too many careless moves, and just like that— Cliff was done.

That was our unspoken warning: don't get too comfortable. Most of us learned fast—keep your mouth shut, answer only when spoken to, follow instructions like a robot on training wheels. If you're a martial arts black belt or a crack shot, keep it under wraps. The academy isn't a stage to shine—it's a hurdle to clear.

Show off, and you'll just make the bar higher for yourself.

We were running today—three miles. Like my high school track days, running was my escape, a few precious minutes away from the crowd, a time just to breathe and be alone. Oneta was last again. As the first three of us crossed the finish line, we turned around to bring her in. It was always expected—we went back for the last one. A lesson in patience, in life.

Back in the locker room, her face was streaked red and white from effort and tears. I helped her into the shower to cool down.

"Becca, I think I've got most of it... except the Wall," she gasped between broken breaths. "I can't get over it. Four months till the physical test. Can you help me?"

"Of course, Oneta. We all have to help each other through," I said, handing her a cold washcloth.

But inside, I felt horribly conflicted. Secretly, I hoped she wouldn't make it. We all did. Because if she passed? She'd be the most dangerous and utterly useless backup you could have in a bar fight.

When we got back to the classroom, there was a new instructor waiting—one we hadn't heard from yet. He was a big man, the kind whose presence filled the room before he said a word. His humor was dark, the kind you earn by escaping death a few too many times.

He launched straight into it: the most dangerous person you'll meet on the street? A parolee. Not because they're always bad—but because they're desperate. "They'll do anything," he said, "*anything* not to go back to prison. Including kill."

Chapter Five: Jewels in Heaven

Then, to drive it home, he rolled up his sleeve and held out his arm. A thick scar—wide and angry—ran along his flesh like a grim exclamation point.

"That," he said calmly, pointing to the scar, "was a parolee who didn't want to go back."

He let it sink in, then continued, pacing slowly.

"Listen up—if you think people are gonna love you because you're a cop? Slap that out of your melon right now. Nobody loves cops. People love firefighters. Everyone loves firefighters. Their mission is simple—FIRE. You call, they show up, spray some water, save a kitten, and everyone cheers. They're the heroes in the calendar.

"You? You're the sheepdog.

"People—the public—they're the sheep. Harmless, mostly. But your job is to keep the wolf away. When the wolf's near? They love you. They cling to you. They bake you pies.

"But the second that wolf disappears? The sheep forget. They wander; they push boundaries. That's when you have to nip at their heels, keep them in line.

"And that's when they hate you.

"That's the job. That's how you're seen. So if you're in this for gratitude or glory? You're in the wrong uniform."

He wrapped up his talk the way to my heart: by handing out a book. Not just any book—*The Gift of Fear* by Gavin de Becker.

"Read this," he said, holding it up like scripture. "And if you've got women in your life—get them a copy, too."

A free book? I liked this guy.

I read it cover to cover in a few days, borderline obsessed. Turns out, the title wasn't metaphorical—*fear* really is a gift. Not the kind that ruins your weekend or makes you cancel plans, but the sharp kind. The kind that raises the hairs on your neck when someone gives you that *off* feeling in a parking garage. The kind that doesn't need a PowerPoint or an explanation—just your attention.

Some people call it gut instinct. Others call it common sense. I call it the one voice in your life that always has your back and never borrows money. Ignore it at your own peril—it doesn't yell, but it sure knows when to whisper.

The final month arrived like the last mile of a marathon—equal parts adrenaline, exhaustion, and questioning all your life choices. We'd started with a full roster, but by then, seven were gone—some flamed out, some fizzled quietly, and one just stopped showing up after a particularly unfortunate turn at weaponless defense.

But somehow, Oneta was still with us.

She'd passed everything but *The Wall*—that dreaded six-foot plank of judgment sitting smugly at the heart of the course. Every cadet had to conquer it to graduate. No exceptions, no do-overs. Just you, your legs, and gravity's cold indifference.

A week before graduation, it was Oneta's last shot. We lined the edge of the field like spectators at a gladiator match, collectively holding our breath. She rounded the corner, face set in determination, legs churning. We all whispered prayers—some for her success, others (if we're honest) for her failure.

She reached the wall, sprang upward—and froze.

Chapter Five: Jewels in Heaven

Her fingers barely grazed the top before her body betrayed her, slumping back down in a dusty heap. For a moment, no one moved. She sat on the ground, legs splayed, dignity dented. Then she stood up, brushed herself off, and walked over to the sergeant.

"I want to thank you for the opportunity," she said, loud enough for us all to hear.

Then she turned to us—her classmates, her almost-peers—and gave a small nod of gratitude. And just like that, she walked off the field. No tears, no drama, no second attempt. Just a quiet exit stage left. It was… noble, in its own way. Like watching someone realize, mid-audition, that Broadway's not for them—and still curtsy before they leave.

We never saw her again. But to this day, when I see a Frappuccino or someone struggling with a six-foot wall—figurative or otherwise—I think of Oneta, and the guts it takes to walk away with grace.

I took a moment to soak it all in—the whole absurd, exhausting, beautiful mess of it. Most of us were young, and those who weren't young in years were still green in the ways that mattered. We were learning to face down our biggest adversary: ourselves. Our doubts, our mental blocks, our "I could never's"—getting stripped away, repackaged into "maybe I can," and eventually, "hey, I just did."

Watching someone finally pass the range or scramble over that cursed wall? Pure electricity. We all felt it—cheering like proud parents at a T-ball game. And when someone failed, it hit us, too. The disappointment wasn't theirs alone—we carried it together, in sweaty solidarity.

We cared about each other. Deeply. And in that unforgiving place of drills, dirt, and emotional whiplash, those moments of shared humanity were our jewels in heaven.

Chapter Six

Messes

Late spring in the Livermore Valley had a smell—sun-warmed grass, pencil shavings, and kids teetering on the edge of excitement, ready for summer vacation to begin. Mom did not much like public school and used to say, "I don't get my children back until the end of June; that is when I start to recognize all of you again." It took four solid weeks of summer break just to detox us from nine months of public school—four weeks to unwind the sass, the squabbles, and the odd behaviors we picked up like lint from the carpet of institutional life.

But by August? Oh, we were delightful once again, or at least she thought so. Calm. Curious. Sweet-natured, like woodland creatures who'd been gently reintroduced into the wild. That's when she recognized us again—the kids she actually liked.

She never had much faith in the public school system. "When in life," she'd ask, "are you ever locked in a room with 25 people your exact same age?" It's a fair point. The whole setup felt less like social development and more like a petri dish of pettiness—constant picking, bickering, and competition, with barely a life skill in sight.

The first week of summer vacation was my weekend at Grandma's house. She never babysat all eight of us at once—she wasn't a saint, just Portuguese—but every now and then, she'd take one or two of us overnight to give Mom a breather. I was posted up outside the school, backpack hanging off one shoulder like I'd just survived a tour of duty. When Grandma's big yellow Buick came into view, I didn't wait. As soon as the tires slowed, I yanked the door open and dove into the back seat like a kid escaping a hostage situation.

"Becca! I almost ran you over!" Grandma wheezed, one hand on the wheel, the other clutching her chest like she was about to meet the Blessed Mother.

"Sorry," I said, already sprawling across the seat like a refugee from third grade.

Getting away from our big, loud, elbow-throwing Italian Catholic family was heavenly. Even if Grandma could be a little heavy on rules and light on dessert, her house was calm, quiet, and—blessedly—free of sibling brawls.

Grandma was a Portuguese Catholic woman with a sharp eye for style and a wardrobe that always seemed one silk scarf ahead of the trends. It's easy to see where my mother got her flair—grace ran in their veins, though neither of them ever made a fuss about it. Grandma worked as a secretary, tapping away at a typewriter to support her two daughters after her husband, Harold, vanished from the family story like a chapter torn out mid-sentence.

We were told he was an inventor—came up with the original umbrella tent design—and a deep-sea diver, which sounded impressive. Apparently, family life didn't sit well with him. He had what they called a "restless spirit," which was the family's polite way of saying he packed up and left one day.

While Grandma worked at a local book company, the nuns looked after the girls. According to Mom, Grandma never com-

Chapter Six: Messes

plained about Harold running off. She just offered it up to the Lord, kept her head down, and stayed busy. The most she ever muttered was a quiet, "That sorry S.O.B.," usually under her breath while scrubbing a dish or ironing a blouse with a little more steam than necessary.

She had work to do. Children to raise. A life to keep moving, one steady step at a time.

Anyway, we had Grandma—and somehow, that was always enough.

Grandmas are supposed to smell like food—and she did. Mostly bacon and coffee, which she adored. The only meat she loved more was Linguica. When it was "on special" at the butcher shop, she never missed the chance to stop by and pick some up.

One warm Friday evening, I saw a side of Grandma I'd never seen before. The butcher was waiting for her, the Linguica already wrapped in butcher paper and tied with string, like a gift. I watched as he slid the cold package across the counter, slow and deliberate, until their hands met for the briefest moment. She looked up at him and gave the prettiest smile—soft, a little shy, but certain.

I stood there blinking, suddenly aware that Grandma wasn't just a grandma. She was a woman. A beautiful one. I never knew why nothing more ever came of that moment, but something in me knew—it had meant something, at least once.

Grandma lived in a 1930s Spanish Mission-style apartment complex—a half-moon of ten tiny cottages wrapped around a central courtyard, each one with its own little porch and flowerbed, like something from a storybook.

We pulled up to the back entrance and climbed the three concrete steps to her kitchen door. The screen creaked as she pulled it open, groceries balanced on one hip. With one foot, she propped the screen, unlatched the door with her free hand, and in a graceful twist of timing and muscle memory, slipped inside without letting the screen slap her on the behind. She did it in one motion—fluid, practiced, unbothered.

The whole studio apartment couldn't have been more than six hundred square feet, but Grandma kept it spotless. Everything had its place. In the kitchen sat an old white Frigidaire, the kind with rounded corners and a handle you had to yank. On top of it perched her ceramic rooster and hens, a little flock that had been keeping watch for at least thirty years. Like the Mona Lisa, no matter where you stood, those chicken eyes seemed to follow you.

The rest of the apartment was just as charming and compact as the kitchen. Every room featured those classic Spanish-style archways—curved doorways leading from the cozy dining room, down the narrow hall, all the way to the tiny bathroom.

The hall had one of those old-fashioned hot air grates—the kind Marilyn Monroe famously posed over—and we loved to imagine ourselves as her, giggling in our nightgowns as the warm air danced around us.

The main living room boasted a large square window framed by lush white hydrangeas just outside, filling the space with a soft, garden-like glow. On either side of the room sat a daybed: one for Grandma, and the other usually reserved for a grandchild spending the night.

Chapter Six: Messes

She turned to me this particular day and yawed and said, "Let's take a nap." Funny how the sight of us kids seemed to make her tired. Actually, I felt tired too from a full day of school, so I did not fuss much about taking a nap. She opened the door and let the breeze blow in. The distant wind chimes created a peaceful rhythm that had us asleep in no time. I woke up only an hour later to the smell of Linguica and coffee and ladies' voices, urging each other to be quiet because Becca was asleep. It was Mom and Grandma, quietly going back and forth, sharing and laughing. That silence was soon broken by a crash through the back door, Blaise had entered the room, followed closely by Vincent.

"Oh gosh, why did Mom have to bring them?" I pulled the blanket over my head but peeked out from under the fuzz to spy on their argument.

Through the blurry veil of blanket fibers, I could just make out Vincent standing in the middle of the living room. It looked like he'd shaved the ends of his eyebrows, so they angled upward—like his hero Spock from *Star Trek*. Spock was all nerves of steel, logic over emotion, and it made sense Vincent wanted to channel that calm power.

But Blaise? He was clearly not amused. Vincent adopting Spock's persona gave him some sort of upper hand over Blaise, who was just itching to explode.

I wasn't sure about the whole shaved-eyebrow thing though. It felt... a little too weird. Hmm. This could get interesting.

So, I stayed hidden under my blanket, watching.

Blaise bellowed something venomous. Vincent, calm as ever, raised one shaved eyebrow and said, "Emotions are illogical."

That sent Blaise into a rage. He charged after Vincent into the kitchen—the very same kitchen where Mom and Grandma were quietly enjoying their Linguica.

"Definitely not a good choice," I thought just as a steaming piece of Linguica came flying through the air, splatting messily against the far wall.

Vincent ducked without missing a beat, raising the other eyebrow this time. "Humans are illogical."

But Mom and Grandma? They were the ones who truly lost it.

As the Camp-a-lot bounced and crept its way up and down the Napa Valley hills, we must've left in such a hurry that the cupboards weren't latched. Big mistake. Soon, things started making a break for it.

This wasn't exactly news to us—cupboard chaos was kind of a family tradition. One of us would launch into superhero mode: dive, catch the rogue jar mid-flight, toss it back in like a pro, and slam the door shut—all before the bus hit the next curve and your stomach did a little flip.

But if too many cupboards were left open and everything turned into flying projectiles? That's when the real fun began. You'd throw your hands over your head, curl into a tight little ball, and pray to every saint you knew that the flying cans didn't find their mark—because, honestly, that bus wasn't stopping anytime soon.

Grace, my older middle sister, was determined to be Mom's favorite. Being the middle child—and middle girl—she often felt invisible, so she made it her personal mission to stand guard. Usually, she was the first to leap from her seat and snag whatever was

Chapter Six: Messes

about to hit the floor. I tried once to compete for Mom's attention this way, but disaster struck. We both dove for the same falling object and bonked heads. After that, I wisely handed over the job to her. She earned the title "Grace the Catcher," and wore it like a badge of honor.

I was sitting on the long couch behind the driver when I spotted the sharp hairpin turn up ahead. Just then, I heard the pantry door creak ominously. I knew it wasn't going to hold.

Sure enough, as the bus leaned into the curve, the cupboard door swung wide open. The sack of rice was the first to make a break for it, hanging precariously on the edge of the shelf, slowly spilling its contents in a steady, unstoppable drizzle. And to make matters worse, just seconds before, a bottle of Aunt Jemima syrup had made its own escape.

"Moooooom!" came the shout, finger jabbed toward the chaos.

She sprang up, hands bracing against the swaying bus walls, but the bus wasn't done yet. With a sudden lurch, balance gave way, and down she came with a thud. She lay there, waiting for a straight stretch of highway to right herself and then, without missing a beat, she reached for the swinging pantry door and said in her usual calm tone, "Well, we'll just have to clean it up when we park."

Somewhere between the thud and the spill, it was clear: the mess wasn't the only thing that would need tending when we parked. The next morning, just as sleep was loosening its grip, my nose was the first to wake up right on time to be assaulted by the unmistakable whiff of septic. Dad was the only one who could drive the bus, and it needed to be hauled off to the dump station. Of course, he wouldn't be back until later in the day.

I sat up, rubbing the sleep from my eyes, and looked around. Everyone else? Gone. Just me and the lingering stink. Perfect. What a fine family, leaving me to enjoy the aroma solo.

Stepping outside, I found Mom crouching over the picnic table changing a diaper on a baby that wasn't hers,. It belonged to the young couple camping nearby.

"Mom, what are you doing with that baby?"

She looked up, calm as ever. "His parents needed a break. I told them, 'No problem—I'll babysit. You go have some alone time.'"

She had a Louis Armstrong eight-track playing, and *La Vie en Rose* floated softly through the air—"hold me close" crooning in that deep, smoky voice. She swayed the baby gently, rocking in slow circles. The hem of her dress whispered *swoosh, swoosh* against the floor as her ankles cracked softly, shifting weight back and forth, back and forth, like a quiet dance just for two.

As she danced that quiet dance of love for children, she reached out and handed me the dirty diaper.

"Shhh, now Becca," she whispered, "take this over to the trash bin over there."

I wasn't sure what was worse—the septic smell or the diaper itself. How could she stand it? Moms have this superhuman ability to handle messes like no one else.

I grabbed the diaper with two fingers of disgust, flung it into a nearby trash can and made a beeline for the edge of the campsite—the first real breath of fresh air I'd had since waking up.

Chapter Six: Messes

Blaise spotted me coming and immediately hissed, "Shhh! You'll scare him!" He was on a serious mission: hunting the great Horny Toad lizard—the little critter famous for squirting blood out of its eyes when it's mad. Tough little armored warriors, covered in thorny scales like tiny prehistoric tanks. Blaise loved chasing them just for the thrill, then, mercifully, letting them go.

He even taught me how to hunt lizards, though only the Blue Bellies. Not as fast, not as deadly, basically the training wheels of lizard hunting.

The trick to catching one? You had to wave your hand in front of the lizard like a stop sign to block its escape route, then scoop it up from behind before it darted off. You had to avoid grabbing the tail at all costs—because that tail detaches like a bloody, squirming getaway artist, leaving you clutching a lizard-shaped horror show.

And then there were the tiny feet, scrambling and spinning like they were auditioning for *Dancing with the Stars*. Most people would freak out and let go right then and there. Girls especially. But I wasn't most people. When I went lizard hunting, I gritted my teeth, held on, determined to prove I had what it took.

"SSSSShhh! You'll scare him!" Blaise warned again, barely able to contain himself. "Quick—go over there! I found a Horn Toad!"

I slipped into position, blocking the lizard's getaway like a pro. He was lightning fast. Blaise's hands moved so quickly I barely saw them. Then he yelled, triumphant, "Got him! Got him!"

But seconds later he screamed like a little girl. Blaise stumbled out from behind the boulders, lizard blood smeared all over his face, his hands empty. The Horny Toad had vanquished the boy and not the other way around.

Finding a private corner on that bus was like trying to catch smoke with your bare hands. As a kid, I wasn't out there hunting for my own identity. It was more like being part of a very loud, slightly chaotic herd. The littlest ones belonged to someone else's orbit; their stories tangled up in bigger siblings or busy parents.

But Elizabeth? She was at that tipping point—old enough to want out but stuck in the bus's tight squeeze. She wasn't built for bus life anyway. With her striking, noble Pocahontas vibe and knowing glances, she was like a rare bird stuck in a noisy aviary. It didn't help that she constantly fought with Mom.

"You're not going out looking like that," Mom would say, voice full of that mix of exasperation and authority only moms have. "And no, you can't stay out till midnight. I don't care what time it's over."

Elizabeth would roll her eyes so hard it was a wonder they didn't get stuck.

On and on it went—Elizabeth lobbying for a date, Mom refusing like it was a matter of national security. But finally, late that summer, Mom caved and approved one. Elizabeth was *thrilled*. She spent the entire day preparing like she was heading to prom... or battle. Maybe both.

She disappeared into the tiny bus bathroom and stayed so long the entire hallway fogged up like a sauna. Steam poured from the top of the door like she was boiling pasta in there. When she finally emerged, her long dark hair was brushed to a high-gloss shine—smooth, thick, and swishy, like a prize-winning horse's tail. I was dying to pet it, but even I knew better than to get that close to the queen in her war paint.

Chapter Six: Messes

Her cubby was near the top, bigger than anyone else's, an unspoken perk of being the oldest and the prettiest. Clothes flew in every direction: tops, scarves, jeans, shoes. She'd hold something up, sigh dramatically, toss it aside, and repeat. It was a one-woman fashion show with an audience of none and the stakes of a royal wedding.

At last, she emerged from the bedroom like a phoenix rising straight out of a disco inferno—rocking a skin-tight halter top, bell-bottoms she'd chopped into denim underwear, and platform shoes so high she looked like she could dunk a basketball. She clomped down the bus steps with the grace of a giraffe on roller skates, hips swaying like she was auditioning for *Soul Train.*

I was curled up in the corner like a wise old owl, barely blinking, already seeing the mess coming like a slow-motion train wreck. The women in our family had spent generations crafting proper ladies—corset-wearing, thank-you-note-writing, chin-up-and-cross-your-ankles kind of ladies. And here she was, teetering into the night like the opening act for regret.

Just when I thought she'd gotten away clean, Mom's voice rang out—sharp, righteous, and louder than a record scratch in a silent room: "You are *not* going out there dressed like that."

Busted!

The evening Dad finally came home and drove the bus to the dump station, we were all grateful—for him, and for the return of breathable air. You'd think by now there'd be some kind of warning system for when a septic tank was nearing disaster, especially in a bus packed with this many people. But no. It always crept up on us... quietly, then all at once.

It made me wonder—why do people wait until something becomes a full-blown, nose-wrinkling mess before they do something about it?

Quickly scribbling in my notebook:

"Sometimes life's just a big stinky mess—like dealing with septic tanks, dirty diapers, and wrong outfit choices—but maybe that mess is helping us get ready for something awesome, like becoming a superhero who can handle anything"… Maybe…

The books had taken over. What started as a neat stash under the bed had become a leaning tower of paper—notes, novels, journals—one sneeze away from collapse. Time for bookcase.

Just Lorenzo came with me. The kids—still technically "kids," though taller than me and constantly hungry—opted out. The older two were lost in high school schedules, and Andrea, our seventh-grade CEO, managed her world with a clipboard and color-coded pens.

I'd braced for teenage rebellion—slammed doors, eye rolls, speeches about freedom—but it never showed. Their lives were too packed: school, ballet, soccer, Disneyland. Repeat. No time for angst.

They had everything—two working parents, orthodontics, clean sheets, and dinners that came with garnish. We wanted them safe, fed, and aiming high. Maybe the White House. Maybe a convent.

Chapter Six: Messes

When they drifted, it wasn't far. A raised eyebrow from me, and the chore chart filled in like magic—always in pen.

Then one night at dinner, after I finished telling a story from my bus-living, barefoot-childhood days, Andrea looked up thoughtfully.

"Our life is kind of boring," she said. "I wish we were poor like you."

And there it was—the kind of secure childhood that lets you romanticize struggle. A strange guilt settled quietly in my chest, like an old memory I hadn't asked to feel. Structured hardship, purposeful, formative stress that built strength and character was what I was after for these kids, not random, chaotic suffering that broke people down. The truth was, Dad bought the bus because he could not afford a new travel van, so he made do with what he had, his brains and brawn. That was the ingenuity message I wanted them to take away. She was too young to understand, I reasoned.

But her question did make me think, long deep and hard about today, this moment in time: *We wish we were poor like you and lived on a bus.*

Had life really become that mundane? My mind began to wander far far away……

I left the Police Academy full of fire. Now I'm a bailiff—eight to five, weekends off—a life measured in quiet rhythms and broken vending machines.

The girl who dreamed of adventure is boxed away, while my daughters blaze their own bright trails.

TV shows make cops glamorous, flawless warriors. Reality? It's the ordinary days—the planning, the patience, the steady work—

that hold real magic. It reminded me of a G.K. Chesterton quote, "The ordinary family is the most extraordinary thing."

Hardship and beauty entwined, perhaps if we honored the struggle, kids wouldn't wish for bus rides and poverty, but see the grace in quiet, steady life.

Dragging myself home after a long day at work I saw that *Lorenzo* had made Tuna Helper for dinner, the kind with only three peas in the box. He was proud that he could help and as my son came in through the back door and sat at the table, Lorenzo made sure to capture all three peas as he scooped up a ladle of it and plopped it on our son's dinner plate.

"Where are the girls?" I asked Lorenzo.

He glanced up from the table, "Dropped Andrea at soccer, Alisha at ballet."

For Lorenzo, juggling dinner and shuttle duty was nothing short of Tesla inventing alternating current—impressive, rare, and slightly miraculous. Bless him, he tried, and that was enough for me because he hadn't touched a drop of alcohol in years. However, the old demons still lurked in the shadows. When I gently nudged him about getting help to face those ghosts, he bristled. The conversation spiraled into an argument, so I let it go.

These were our good years—my bar had sunk pretty low—just having someone in the house who didn't abuse alcohol felt like a victory. No more hearing, "Hey, you better drink these winecoolers, they have been sitting in the fridge for a week; they are about to go bad."

Chapter Six: Messes

Or the routine morning proclamation: "Could you whisper? Loud voices hurt my ears. Plus, I focus better with one eye closed and sleeping on the floor is way more comfortable."

A new janitor, Joni, had just started her morning shift at the courthouse, tackling the usual—cleaning bathrooms while people streamed in and out all day. She'd placed the "Restroom Closed" sign on the men's room door when, suddenly, a man furious about a judge's ruling shoved past her and started peeing all over the floor. He was taking out his anger in the worst possible way.

Joni came and found me, told me what happened as my eyes became wide with disbelief. I was seething, not just at the mess, but at the disrespect. In my mind, if you peel back every wrong in this world, it boils down to one thing: lack of respect.

I stepped into the bathroom while he was mid-stream, and for some reason, the words, "Drop it," slipped out of my mouth, which to my surprise he did and foisted his hands up in the air. So, I just went with it.

"You know this janitor isn't responsible for the judge's decision. The judges don't even use this bathroom—they each have their own in chambers. Now, clean up your mess and apologize to Joni."

He blinked, swallowed, and—somehow—complied.

I used her name on purpose—to humanize her in that moment. Inside, I was silently begging, *please don't argue.* To my relief, he didn't. He cleaned up his mess, borrowed her cleaner, apologized, and left the courtroom.

Joni stood behind me, mouth agape and eyes wide. After the man left, she whispered, "That's the nicest thing anyone has ever done for me."

We became friends after that. Despite the wear etched into her hands and body from years of hard work, her eyes were bright—joyful in a way that contradicted the story her hands told. A photographer friend once said you can capture beauty in the eyes alone, even if the face is plain. They truly are the windows to the soul—and Joni's soul shone through hers.

I liked her instantly. Soon, when she came into the courthouse, you could hear our laughter echoing through the halls. As I learned her story of journey from bad relationships and drug abuse to a life recaptured and rebuilt, I began to not only see my own troubles in a new light but those in an industry I had never thought about before, janitors. Those invisible souls who keep buildings spotless. Most people don't give a second thought to those who clean the floors or empty the trash, people just expect the buildings they work in to be clean every morning. Meanwhile, people stomp in with muddy shoes, toss trash carelessly, and sometimes break things on purpose. Day after day, janitors witness the same lack of respect.

At night, under cover of darkness, janitors wash, scrub, mop, and empty—quiet ghosts holding everything together. The ones cleaning during the day? They are invisible. Ironically, I would have my judge make me let Joni in to clean her chambers while meeting with lawyers in high profile cases thinking nothing of her as a person that would over-hear their conversation.

Chapter Six: Messes

Cleaning out a trash can one day, Joni looks up and me and says, "No one grows up dreaming of being a janitor,"

As she tied up the heavy trash bag, it suddenly became symbolic of her life and others who create messes of their lives.

I was remembering nights at the jail supervising female trustees, who spoke in hushed whispers sharing their stories with each other. Broken home this, battered that, and then there was that man. They all seemed to run into the same guy, charming and who loved them conditionally, as long as they agreed to deliver drugs or whatever. They would each acquiesce, get caught, and then have their children taken away by Child Protective Services—nothing funny about that.

Now, stuck in the criminal justice system, they needed a job if they ever wanted their children back—and janitorial services were always hiring.

Joni, toughened by her own similar stories, had her own way of handling people who pushed their luck—usually quiet, deliberate, and oddly effective. Her humor wasn't for show; it was a kind of armor, polished by years of watching nonsense walk through courtroom doors.

One spring, a trio of teenage girls stood trial for vandalizing the high school. During recesses, they'd crowd into the courthouse restroom, pull out tubes of bright red lipstick, and leave kiss marks all over the mirrors—layers of greasy, self-satisfied graffiti.

Joni had just finished cleaning one morning when she saw them heading in again, laughing like they had nothing to answer for. She followed them in, said nothing, just walked past, dipped her rag into the toilet, and calmly wiped it across the mirror, smearing away their handiwork.

The girls stared, mouths open.

"This is how I clean the mirrors," Joni said, glancing at their reflections. "Pretty efficient, don't you think?"

They shrieked and scrambled out, nearly knocking me over in the hallway.

Watching people come and go out of the courthouse had a way of stirring thoughts in me. Women like Joni came into focus—strong, capable, and sharp-edged—but once, a long time ago, they were young girls, too, with dreams not so different from anyone else's. Life had unfolded into a series of messes, each one demanding attention, each one quietly pushing some hope further out of reach. Likely the same was true for my mother. Dreams, unspoken and unlived, probably sat somewhere beneath the surface of her days.

Thoughts circled back to personal ground. Dreams left undone. College came to mind—once a goal, now a closed door, sealed by geography and responsibility. Yet something lighter tugged at memory's edge, not a duty, not a regret—just a longing that had never quite let go.

A horse.

Funny how one little word—*no*—can echo through the years like a slammed door in a quiet hallway.

"No, Becca, you *cannot* have a horse," my mother had declared, and just like that, the dream was shelved. For decades, I carried that shut-down answer like a rule carved in stone. I never even questioned it.

Chapter Six: Messes

Horse? Of course, not.

Sure, there are "women comforts," but none seemed to fill that hollow spot in my heart, Spa Day? Nope, I don't like to be touched. Nails? That is not me. I just wasn't one of those women who enjoyed those things. Reasoning, I didn't ask for much—just worked, worried, and did my best to stay upright.

Then at that very moment, lost in thought, I realized as if for the very fist time, "Hey, wait a minute, I was a grown-up."

A real one. With keys, a mortgage, and the ability to say *yes* to myself. And what did I want, more than anything? That horse. That *darn* horse I'd dreamed of since I was nine with skinned knees and sticker burrs in my socks.

Once the decision was made, the universe didn't dawdle. Saying my dream out loud to a friend, I got a call back less than a week later, "I got one for you, and his name is Zack."

Twelve years old, seventeen hands tall, the color of coffee with a splash of cream. A dark chestnut Thoroughbred with eyes so kind you'd swear he knew your whole life story. Elegant, gentle, beautifully trained, he looked like something you'd win in a fairy tale or find on the cover of a romance novel.

I had zero real horse experience. I only knew I loved the smell of them. Yet, with even less hesitation, I handed over twelve hundred dollars to his owner, and he was mine.

Horse people understand—there's something about the outside of a horse that reaches straight into a person's soul. Zack had that effect. On my days off from work, the car practically drove itself down the gravel lane to the boarding stable, past white fences and sun-dappled oaks, where horses grazed like something out of my childhood experience of Napa Valley. The place had a rhythm, a quiet hum that made even an ordinary Tuesday feel like a vacation.

But having Zack was not without its obstacles. Turns out, *having* and *wanting* are two very different things. The smell I had no idea about was horse urine. It has a special brand of potency that could peel paint. The manure—runny, relentless—was no better. And somehow, cleaning it all took just as long as riding did. Add hauling hay bales, mixing supplements, brushing out mud-caked coats, worming schedules, and writing checks to the farrier every six weeks—it all added up, fast. Time, money, sore muscles... none of it had made it into my childhood fantasy.

But then we'd hit the trail. Just the two of us winding through the hills, the rhythm of his hooves steady beneath me, the sun slicing through the trees. Out there, the world softened. The muck, the money, the mess—they faded behind the sound of breathing and hoofbeats, and the grounding, beautiful scent of him—the warm, leathery, unmistakable smell of horse. In that moment, I remembered exactly why I'd said yes.

Entry into my notebook:

"Sometimes, without warning, tears come—not from sadness exactly, but from that strange ache beauty leaves behind when it brushes up against something half-forgotten. Maybe that's what horses do best—carry more than just a rider."

Chapter Seven

Celebration

Since it was America's Bicentennial—the big two hundredth birthday—Mom decided it was high time the men in our family got patriotic. Not that she came up with the idea herself. It started, as many things did in our lives, in the church parking lot.

She met a retired Marine colonel after Mass—Colonel Max Madson, a man who looked like he could still win a war with one hand tied behind his back. He was forming a Fife and Drum Corps to perform across the Western United States in celebration of America's birthday, and he just *happened* to mention he needed a few more men.

Mom, never one to let an opportunity pass—or let her boys off the hook—volunteered our entire male population on the spot.

Dad wandered up mid-recruitment, shook the Colonel's hand like he was accepting a Medal of Honor, and declared what an honor it would be to join such a once-in-a-lifetime endeavor.

The conversation outside the church stretched on for what felt like the entire Revolutionary War. Everyone else had long gone home. We kids sat on the bench, swinging our legs and listening to the Colonel's deep, gravelly voice paint scenes of musket fire, tattered flags, and fifes playing through the smoke.

He spoke of the battles—how the music had roused weary soldiers, kept them marching, kept them *fighting*. Without the fife and drum, he said, they might've lost not only the war, but also their nerve. Some Corps members had stood their ground without weapons, just rhythm and courage, and many had died doing it.

"Unfortunately," the Colonel continued, "the tradition fell into disuse after the First World War."

He said it with such regret, you'd think he'd watched it happen himself. His Corps had five dedicated men—but life, as it does, often got in the way. Illness, work schedules, family obligations... he needed more bodies. Preferably those who could hold a beat and show up on time.

The fact that Dad had a bus—and a whole crew of boys—made the Colonel visibly brighten. You could almost see the gears turning as he looked at our family and saw not just reinforcements, but a rolling, ready-made band.

And just like that, we were in.

Before you could say "Uncle Sam," our family was touring California with a Fife and Drum Corps, riding high in Dad's old school bus, its seats now filled with instruments, uniforms, and the smell of brass polish.

The first day of practice, we headed to Colonel Madson's house—a place that looked exactly like where a retired Marine would live. Perched at the top of a hill, it had a wide wraparound porch, heavy oak doors, and a sense that everything inside had a purpose.

His wife, Abby, greeted us with a kind smile and the quiet confidence of someone who'd hosted many young recruits, whether military or musical. When she opened the door, the first thing that hit you was the library—floor-to-ceiling books, packed tight like soldiers in formation. At the far end stood a grand, carved desk positioned in front of a panoramic window that framed the mountains and valley like a living painting.

It didn't feel like a room so much as a command center. The Colonel's war room.

Military regalia filled every corner—medals, polished munitions, brass nameplates, and framed documents that looked like they'd been handled by presidents. Flags hung on every wall: the original thirteen colonies on one side, the modern stars and stripes on the other, each displayed with meticulous pride.

Stealing a quick glance at the current flag, I flicked my eyes quickly, but that is all it took for the Colonel to notice it and direct a long-winded history lesson to just me.

"You know," he began, locking eyes, "there are thirteen stripes, alternating red and white, to honor the thirteen colonies that fought for independence and became the first thirteen states."

His voice was steady, practiced—like someone who'd told this story many times and still found pride in every word. "And the fifty stars? One for each state in the union. We've held steady since Hawaii joined in 1959. The current design was adopted on July 4th, 1960. But before that? There were at least twenty-seven versions of the flag—some with more stars, some with fewer, and a few with different numbers of stripes, depending on the era."

He paused, not for applause, but maybe to let the weight of it all settle. It was fascinating—at least for the first couple of minutes. I tried my best to look interested. Blaise, however being the most pugilistic of mom's children, was riveted. Out of all of us, he was the one who genuinely loved war stories. While the rest of us eyed the nearest exit or the tray of cookies, he leaned in, hanging on every word. I think he fell in love with the Colonel right then and there.

Blaise, Vince, and Little Andy were assigned to play the snare drums, Marc, already his High School Drum Major, played that role. Paul played the Fife. Dad, because he was good at banging at things and could not play an instrument, was made the bass drum drummer.

"Hey, I can do this," he beamed as he smashed the sides of the big bass drum with the mallets.

And so, the practice began, Yankee Doodle was the first piece they would learn. The night was long, and I fell asleep on one of the couches in an adjacent living room until Dad shook me, "It's time to go" he said.

We all left that night and got into the car and drove home, and I had this odd feeling—I think it was pride. Proud to be part of this family and of a bigger family called the United States.

About a week later, trouble arrived in the name of Howard Darby. He was the same age as Blaise and had the same sense of mischievous humor and a desire to upset everything that everyone put right. They were a force from Hell.

The bus was full—every seat taken, every aisle crammed with brass and percussion, the air thick with anticipation and instrument oil. This trip to San Francisco was no ordinary outing; the Fife and Drum crew was opening at a Cubs game, and the weight of it buzzed in the bus.

Needing a break from the long drive, Dad pulled into a small town for a break. A quiet row of shops sat just off the road. Blaise and Howard disappeared into a narrow storefront with a hand-

Chapter Seven: Celebration

painted sign that simply read: *Novelties*. They came back fifteen minutes later, faces flushed with victory, and a small brown paper bag crumpled in Howard's hand.

We rolled on.

About half an hour later, a sudden cry from the back of the bus cut through the low hum of conversation.

"Oh, geez—there's dog poop on one of my vintage snares! *How in the world—?*"

Colonel Madson stood there, stunned, the drum in his hands like something defiled. The bus fell quiet, save for the faint rustling of a paper bag quietly shoved beneath a seat.

Shocked into silence, no one said a word. But Blaise and Howard couldn't quite keep the corners of their mouths still. They collapsed against each other, wheezing, laughter spilling out in wild bursts.

"Aaaggghh—ha—ha—ha!"

Blaise reached down, scooped up the offending dog poop, and began wiggling it in front of the Colonel's face. "Colonel Madson, see? *See?* It's rubber!"

The Colonel blinked. First came the sigh—relief. Then the tightening jaw. Not amused.

Before the Colonel could speak, Mom was already halfway down the aisle. Without breaking stride, she reached for Blaise's ear—an old-school grip that needed no translation. He yelped, the rubber prop forgotten in his hand, as she towed him directly across from her and folded her arms. Her silence said everything.

Blaise slouched into the seat, ears red, still trying not to smile.

The wind, sharp, persistent, and determined to rearrange everyone's hair, was already staging its own performance by the time we arrived at Candlestick Park. We found our seats and settled in, scanning the field for the boys.

From the far edge of the stadium, the youngest marched out first, hoisting a banner for the Fife and Drum Corps. The bright yellow lettering blazed against navy fabric, fluttering like it had somewhere more important to be. The boys, in their slightly-too-large colonial uniforms and tricorn hats, looked like history book illustrations that had wandered off the page—earnest, mismatched, and entirely charming. A few in the crowd gave a chuckle, the kind that says, *this is going to be good.*

Then came Marc, tall and serious, leading with the mace like he'd been born to keep time. Behind him, Dad struck his bass drum with martial precision, while Blaise, Andy, and Vincent followed, snare drums tight and proud, tapping out a rhythm that somehow held the whole windy spectacle together.

Even the wind, for a moment, seemed to pause and listen.

The group came to a halt at the center of the field. Marc raised his mace with the solemnity of a battlefield general. A beat of silence—and then, with a swift downward motion, the fifes sprang to life. The drums followed in perfect time. There was Dad, steady as ever, laying down the pulse: *boom, boom-boom* on the massive bass drum.

As they advanced, the younger boys battled the wind like it was a second opponent. The banner whipped up into their faces again and again, flapping wildly as they wrestled it back down and pushed forward. Gripping both the banner and their oversized

Chapter Seven: Celebration

hats, they looked less like colonial foot soldiers and more like Sister Bertrille from *The Flying Nun*, teetering on the edge of liftoff.

Somehow, they made it to the end of the routine—no one airborne, no casualties. The music stopped.

The announcer's voice cut through the applause: "Let's give them a big round of applause!"

The stadium responded with a roar.

Then, with perfect timing and no pause for sentiment: "Let's—PLAY BALL!"

When the Fife and Drum Corps was invited to perform aboard an aircraft carrier anchored just outside San Francisco, it felt like a moment worth dressing up for. Uniforms were pressed, shoes polished, and Grandma—who needed no invitation when adventure was on the table—decided she'd come along, too.

Before the performance, we were given a tour of the ship. It was less a leisurely stroll and more a navigational exercise: narrow corridors that forced a single-file line, low ceilings that punished posture, and the occasional six-inch floor riser between sections.

Grandma, always loyal to fashion over function, had worn shoes that weren't quite built for combat—or corridors. From the rear of the line, we'd hear her now and then, her voice echoing down the steel hallway:

"Oh, these damn shoes!"

It was oddly reassuring. As long as we could hear her grumbling, we knew she was still upright and still with us.

And then we were introduced to a second tour guide.

He was the kind of man who made dress whites look cinematic—salt-and-pepper hair, crisp posture, and enough medals on his chest to make a small shift in gravity. Grandma, who'd been taking the tour at a measured pace, suddenly picked up remarkable speed. Without comment or apology, she moved herself neatly to the front of the line, right beside him.

He, in turn, offered her his arm every time we approached a raised section divider. She accepted, graciously, with a quiet dignity that suggested this sort of thing happened to her often.

And if you watched closely, you might've noticed she began to slow down slightly—just enough to be helped over every single one.

In Grandma's mind, there were never quite *enough* floor dividers.

The tour came to an end in the ship's galley; we were all fed before the performance. Later that day on the way home, Grandma was unusually quiet. Normally chatting with Mom like a magpie, she instead sat staring out the window, humming to herself, quiet and clearly remembering some distant sweet love.

All that traveling had a way of wearing on everyone. The cramped quarters, the constant hum of wheels on asphalt—it got under our skin. The chorus of complaints echoed through the bus: "Stop that!"

"Leave me alone!"

"Quit it!"

"Blaise, stop making those farting noises!"

And on it went, a steady drumbeat of irritation.

Sometimes, you just have to get off that bus.

Chapter Seven: Celebration

That day, it was Paul who finally snapped. Later, Mom asked him why he'd hit Grace. His answer was simple and surprising: it was the only way to get Dad to stop the bus.

Paul was fifteen—old enough to know better, but apparently not old enough to resist plotting an escape. He noticed Grace sitting quietly in the corner of the bench seat and, with calculated precision, jabbed her in the arm.

"Oooowwwww, he hit me!"

Grace's cry sliced through the tension. Just as Paul had planned, the bus slowed. Dad unclipped his seatbelt, his face set like a thundercloud and started toward the back. But before he'd taken more than three steps, Paul was already moving. He grabbed a duffle bag he'd packed earlier, swung open the emergency rear door, and jumped out. He sprinted into the forest, diving under a pile of leaves, tossing branches over himself like a camouflage expert. Dad stormed off the bus, fury trailing behind him like a storm. He searched long after the sun dipped below the horizon.

For Paul, his impulsive escape quickly turned into a dilemma he hadn't quite anticipated because if he gave up his hiding spot, he'd face Dad's wrath and likely a pulverizing. But if he stayed put too long, the chill and exhaustion would force him to move, thereby risking discovery.

As daylight dwindled, Mom and Dad grew desperate. In a last-ditch effort, they lined us up along either side of the bus, pressed our faces to the windows, and called out his name in unison: "Paul! Paul! Where are you?"

Dad circled up and down the highway, hope waning with the fading sun.

The next morning, worn and frustrated, Dad drove the bus to the police station and gave a description to the officers—but then came the unexpected words: "Um, we've got your son, Mr. Ponsano. He's in a wing of Juvenile Hall."

And just like that, the search ended, and we began the quiet ride home, everyone on their best and most saintly behavior.

When Paul returned, Mom wept quietly, the weight of relief settling over her like a benediction. Like the Prodigal Son finally home, we gathered close and rejoiced.

It was time to stop traveling—time to go home and regroup.

Not long after that day, I found myself on the backyard swing, the chains creaking softly as I pumped my legs back and forth, higher with each pass. The sky was pale, the kind of washed-out blue that comes after too much drama. I needed stillness.

Some of my brothers and sisters were angry with Paul—for running off, for worrying everyone, for the weight he'd added to an already tired bus. Others, like me, weren't so sure. We didn't condone what he'd done, but something about it gnawed at us. We wondered what he was really running from—and if, maybe, we ever wanted to run, too.

For my parents, there had been relief—maybe even a quiet celebration. Paul was home, safe, accounted for. That was enough.

I didn't understand the tangle of feelings we all carried. Guilt, anger, love—they'd all piled in with us on the ride home.

When I asked Mom why everyone seemed to feel something different, she didn't explain. Instead, she handed me a Bible and told me to read Luke 15:11–32.

Chapter Seven: Celebration

"The Parable of the Prodigal Son," she said. "Read that—and you'll understand."

And I did. And slowly, I began to.

Leaning against the wall. Shifting feet. Sit. Stand. Stand. Sit. Rinse. Repeat. Comfort was elusive. Case after case droned on like beige wallpaper… until this one.

The defendant was motioned to the counsel table. Simple enough. But no. She breezed right past me, flicked a hand at my instruction like it was a fruit fly, and wandered straight into *The Well*—that sacred, invisible rectangle between the judge and counsel tables, where only court employees tread. Unauthorized passage is basically high treason.

The judge, Eleanor Price, perched up high, eagle-eyed and ego-prone, glared at me as if to say, "WELL? Aren't you going to stop her?"

A quick arm grab and gentle redirection put our floral outlaw back where she belonged. She barely weighed more than a child. Doe eyed, strawberry-blonde hair cascading down her back, she was dressed in a sheer flowered ankle length dress and Birkenstocks, naturally. The poster child for "wandering into trouble while looking like you're headed to a drum circle."

The judge peered over her glasses and began, "Molly, I have here fifteen unpaid parking tickets. Would you care to explain why?"

Molly stood, adjusted her flowered dress like she was about to deliver an acceptance speech, and launched in.

"Well, Judge, I just feel like this is a *free* country, and we should be able to park wherever we want. Telling me I *can't* do that? Frankly, I find that un-American. Also let me ask *you* something."

The judge blinked. This was not on her bingo card.

"What is money made of? Trees, right? Paper. So technically, it's just fancy tree pulp. They even call it 'fiat currency'—which basically means 'pretend.' And if you look outside, Judge, there are *plenty* of trees. So, if you want your money, maybe… I don't know… go climb a tree and make some yourself?"

Dead silence. Somewhere, a squirrel dropped its acorn in disbelief.

A glance at the judge said it all. Sure, Molly's argument was bold, wildly disrespectful, and teetering on the edge of nonsense—but buried somewhere beneath the flower-child defiance and recycled Econ 101 logic… was a sliver of twisted validity.

Our eyes met. I gave her the universal "better you than me" expression.

The judge, recognizing that Molly wasn't exactly playing with a full deck, cleared her throat and began patiently,

"Molly, you live in the United States. Every country has rules. And those rules… must be obeyed."

Molly returned a blank, wide-eyed stare.

The judge sighed, then appointed Molly a special court counsel. Someone, she decided, needed to gently explain to her that "fiat currency" does not mean you can park like its Woodstock every

Chapter Seven: Celebration

day. The case was continued for an hour—enough time, hopefully, for Molly to find the rest of her marbles.

After lunch break, which for me was usually the highlight of my day, it did get a little more interesting. Switching from criminal to civil cases, in walked my realtor. Civil cases can be common enough in real estate, so I was not surprised to see a realtor, but this was the first time I had seen her here. She was sharply dressed, eloquent, confident, and wealthy. She was six years younger than I was. There were no lawyers used for this small case. She came in prepared and well spoken. After the hearing was over, she invited me to have lunch with her at a little café not far from the courthouse. As we sat, I think I fell in love with her at that moment, figuratively, dear reader. What struck me was that she was so calm and confident, not just well dressed. And although she won her case, it seemed she would have been just as at ease had she lost—simply making a calm mental note to be better prepared next time.

For the longest time, I sat and listened to her explain how she had built her financial empire, four other businesses besides being the owner broker of her real estate office. Rachel was her name, and although she had come from modest means, she learned how money worked. How it was made, kept and grown. She had clawed her way out of the financial darkness that permeated the public school system creating workers not builders.

As I left the café and set out a half mile back to the courthouse to resume my day work as a bailiff, my outlook on work, money, child rearing, retirement, cash flow, marriage, everything changed. It was as if I had the chance to change the trajectory of not only my life, but also that of my children. After all, what could I teach them as a cop, how to do a hair-pull take down? What the difference was between Methamphetamine and Heroine? No, I thought, here was the answer to something better, a way to look up and not down. The chance to be around people who were "doers."

Her words settled over me like a fresh breeze—this was free-market economics explained without jargon, in plain, unapologetic truth.

"Entrepreneurship isn't just about chasing dollars. There's this thing called 'enlightened self-interest,' it's what keeps us moving forward—it motivates, inspires, and gives us what I call joy: a kind of happiness that understands there's pain in the process but chooses to keep going anyway."

"You see, Becca, when you work for yourself, creativity isn't just encouraged, it's essential. Being creative opens doors—to new ideas, new opportunities, and yes, more money. But in government jobs? Creative people get shunted aside like broken pencils. The system demands conformity, a dull sameness. Entrepreneurs and inventors? We're the troublemakers, the nuisances—the ones who shake the boat and make everyone else seasick and so we get retaliated against, but in the free market, we are rewarded for being innovators."

Each concept Rachel enlightened for me became an idea that I had never considered before, each example of being dismissed or criticized for thinking too much or offering my opinion too often or being written up was a familiar and relatable memory that I had buried. And here is where I misunderstood my Catholicism. I accepted that criticism and stayed small because that is what I thought it meant to be a saint. I began to realize that being a saint does not mean putting your head down and accepting abuse. The

Chapter Seven: Celebration

humility the Church teaches is not passivity but the clearing away of ego, so that we can see clearly and act rightly. For much of my life, I mistook humility for shrinking. I became small, obedient, and quiet—so much so that it stifled my growth, my flourishing, and even my ability to create and earn. Yet Aquinas teaches that "humility does not consist in hiding the gifts of God, but in submitting ourselves to Him, and using them for His glory." That truth shattered the false humility I had carried for years, and suddenly I felt free to create the life I wanted.

As the days passed from that day at the coffee shop, the circle I once trusted began to feel more like a corral, not a community. My mind was racing with ideas, but conversations stumbled along, stuck in the mud of the mundane. It hit me like a jolt: *this is what it means to outgrow your friends.*

Suddenly, I was speaking a new language—and no one was fluent. No one but Rachel, my realtor and now my new friend, who didn't flinch when I talked about investing, inflation, monetary policy, and financial freedom like it was a real destination. One new friend and one new spark is all it took. I realized then: knowledge without action is just trivia. So, I circled a date. Freedom—inked onto my calendar. Less than a year away, and I would quit, change my friends, take a job as a realtor, learn how to invest and begin a life that fulfilled my need to learn and grow.

But there was a bigger problem looming—Lorenzo. Getting him onboard had to come first, or all my efforts to improve life might collapse like a Schoolie held together with duct tape and prayers. And, indeed, I had prayed for his sobriety for years, only to be reminded by a priest that prayer is only effective if the person with the problem actually bothers to participate. Some years, Lorenzo cooperated. Some years, he didn't. For me, it was hope, then dashed hope, then hope again, then dashed—like some sadistic cosmic spin cycle.

People say Catholics are co-dependents, apparently because we like obedience and helping others. Please. I wasn't in it for approval—I just wanted him to be sober, a halfway decent dad, and maybe enjoy life without sending me into a panic spiral. Catholic teaching says we love and serve not because we need to, but because God commands it. Being called a co-dependent felt like being called an "edgy" nun. I did the soul-searching thing, just to be sure. Nope. My motives weren't insecurity masquerading as virtue—they were rooted in grace, freedom, and purpose. Still, I had to examine my conscience carefully... for what I was about to do.

A week later, I walked through the front door and found him sprawled in his favorite recliner, the picture of lazy contentment.

"Lorenzo," I declared, wagging a finger like a judge in a courtroom, "you are an alcoholic!"

He barely blinked, grinning. "I'm not an alcoholic," he said. "Alcoholics need a drink. I *already* have one. Ha! Ha!"

Then, with the grace of a cat reclaiming its throne, he shifted just enough to glare at me. "You're blocking my view of the game."

My mind flashed back years earlier on the Camp-a-lot–Paul! The day Paul ran out the back of the bus—he was just crazy to get out and away from his family. And then I thought, why was I trying so hard to keep him on this bus? If he wanted to get off, who was I to try and force him to stay on?

"Not funny, Lorenzo. Twenty-five years is a long time to wait for someone to choose sobriety." My voice was steady, but the edges were frayed.

"I've been honest—with you, with myself, with every priest and therapist we've seen. And the answer keeps circling back to the same place: you don't want to stop. Some women would've walked out years ago. Others would still be here, clinging to their vows like a lifeline. But the truth of the matter has taken shape—clear, heavy, and inescapable. One of us has to go."

"It sure as hell ain't gonna be me!" he snapped, all wounded pride and whiskey breath.

Not flinching,

"I figured you'd say that." Then sliding the envelope across the table, I simply said, "The kids are grown. The only thing left here is a goldfish in a bowl. I rented a small place on the edge of town. You can stay with the fish… or live there while we sort things out."

He just stared, then rose without a word, lit a cigar, and drew on it hard—puffing, pausing, lost in some smoky trance of thought. Each drag seemed an attempt to smother the pain he never faced: the childhood wounds, the string of his betrayals, the years of shrinking from life's demands. I saw it clearer than he ever could.

How does a man-child—unwilling to lead, unwilling to follow—survive?

I watched him nurse the cigar like a pacifier, and any lingering doubt about my decision vanished.

"Well?" I asked, cutting through the haze.

He said, "I will stay here and take care of the goldfish."

"Done!"

I got my things quickly and headed to my small house on the edge of town. It was not really new, but it was new to me. It needed work, a lot of it, but I did not mind, I was finally free. I figured the goldfish would be dead within the week.

My thoughts drifted back to a time long ago, my childhood and Camelot, and I began to write:

"That gleaming dream built on honor, faith, and the fragile thread of loyalty. Were families, like kingdoms, born with noble intentions—hearts set on righteousness—only to be undone by the slow, relentless siege of betrayal, weakness, and time? Was this the fate of all empires built on love—that they echo Arthur's court, shining for a moment, then crumbling under the weight of being human?

If so, why bother?

But I know the answer to that, too. John Paul II had written in his book, *Crossing the threshold of Hope*, "Bother because it matters."

Chapter Eight

One door closes, One door opens

As Dad drove the bus through small towns, Marc had this thing he just had to do. He'd drop down a side window, lift his trumpet to his lips, and blast out the Cavalry Charge and First Call—*"Ta-da-da-dat, da-dah!"* The notes rang out like a bugle on a battlefield, slicing through the still air of sleepy streets.

People on the sidewalks lit up with sheer delight, pausing mid-step to yell, "CHARGE!" Much to our amusement, they *always* did—didn't matter where we were. Sometimes, a whole group would join in, other times just one or two. Once, even a drunk hunched in a doorway stirred from his stupor, cracked one eye open and croaked, "Chaaaarrrggge…" before curling back into his nap.

Aside from entertaining unsuspecting pedestrians on city sidewalks, the bus doubled as a drivers' training vehicle. Grace had just earned her shiny new drivers permit, but with Dad buried in work, he hadn't found time to teach her.

Normally, when one of the older kids turned sixteen, Dad followed a strict routine: he'd haul out a beat-up work truck with a manual transmission, toss a refrigerator box in the bed, and begin the lesson. The rule was simple—if the box tipped during a downshift, you needed more practice.

But time had slipped away from him, and a promise was a promise. So, with no truck and no box, he handed Grace the keys to the bus—*with all of us in it.*

"Come here, Grace—sit next to me in the driver's seat," he said, motioning her over. They began steering together, his hand guiding hers as the bus crept forward.

Then he turned sharply and snapped, "Marc, knock off that blasted horn—you're making Grace nervous!"

Truthfully, the horn was the least of what made us nervous, Grace getting drivers training on the bus is what had us freaked out, but no one questioned Dad when he was in driving-instructor mode. The bus fell quiet as he resumed his post, one hand on the wheel, the other wrapped around his thermos of coffee, eyes ahead. Grace focused, we held our breath, and the engine rumbled on.

Some hours later as Grace eased the bus into the Napa Valley campground, things went smoothly—until it came time to park. Dad, a little too confident in her budding skills, directed her down an ever narrowing road where the trees leaned in like curious onlookers, their branches drooping lower with every foot.

"Please, God," I whispered, "let this be the grand finale of driver's training."

But Dad never knew when to quit.

SCRAAAAPE. The sound of branches dragging across the roof made us all wince.

In a flash, he lunged forward, pushed Grace from the seat—she tumbled to the floor with a thud—and took the wheel himself, as if this near-miss had somehow caught *him* off guard.

Chapter Eight: One door closes, One door opens

The air conditioning unit on top of the bus had collided with the limb of a giant oak. Back and forth, Dad inched the bus, trying to free the massive branch without ripping the AC clean off. The scraping was unbearable—metal on bark, long and loud, echoing through the quiet campground.

Curious campers emerged from their sites, squinting at the spectacle. I was now old enough to feel it—embarrassment creeping in like heat through a cracked window.

Dad finally threw it in park and climbed onto the roof. The branch was too thick to cut, so he called the boys up, and together they rigged a makeshift block-and-tackle system with pulleys and rope, working like a roadside rescue team to pry the oak limb away from the bus.

It took about fifteen minutes—just long enough to win nods of approval from the onlookers. Disaster averted, dignity intact. And really, at that age, that's all that mattered—saving face.

As we settled in, Vincent went straight to his usual spot and began organizing his cubby. He folded everything—shirts, socks, underwear, even his money. We teased him for it, but deep down we were jealous. He always had cash from odd jobs, and somehow, his world stayed neat, tidy, and under control. In a family of loud mechanics and a mom doing her best to keep the chaos in check, Vincent looked as though he'd been dropped in from another planet.

It's strange how someone can feel alone in a big family—but he did. Always looking for a quiet edge to perch on, a little space just for God and him.

Mom called Little Andy, Vincent, and me her "three little ones," bundling us together whether we liked it or not. But Vincent always managed to slip away, orbiting back to her side whenever he could.

And where did Mom always want to be? Church. The only thing that made church bearable for me was the potluck afterward. But to get to the food, you had to survive not just the endless prayers of mass, but Sunday school, too.

I remember one lesson, the teacher droning on like a broken record. "Now, the origins of Catholicism, up until the Reformation, the whole world was Catholic. Blah, blah, blah, Luther—a priest—and a guy named Calvin didn't like the corruption. Blah, blah, blah. More specifically, how church and government had become one and the same, so they protested the corruption, hence the word Protestant."

The words blurred into a fog of history, my stomach rumbling louder and louder soon overtaking both my brain and mouth, I blurted out, "Okay, can we eat now?"

Vincent, sitting beside me, gave my leg a sharp kick. I glanced over—I could not believe it; he was actually taking notes. Perfect, neat, detailed notes.

He wasn't just the teacher's pet; he genuinely liked this grown-up world. If a ten-year-old could admire an eight-year-old, I admired him.

The smell of damp fog crept in with dawn, stirring my conscience awake. I peered out the window of the Camp-a-lot to see a thick haze blanketing the meadow, turning the morning into some-

Chapter Eight: One door closes, One door opens

thing out of an ancient legend—like the battlefield of King Arthur's time.

My mind raced to the thunder of hooves pounding the valley floor, the clash of armor and battle cries. But the real sound was Mom in the kitchen, clanging pots and pans as she readied to feed her army—preparing the breakfast line she would feed that morning.

I rolled out of bed and onto my feet like the warrior I imagined myself to be, marched into the kitchen, and poured a cup of coffee. Mom swooped in and added half a cup of creamer, letting me keep up the illusion of adulthood. I loved her for that.

She put the pots away for a moment, and we curled up on the couch to watch the sun rise over the hill, its light spilling across the meadow, signaling the start of a new day. We had a big one ahead—Vincent's birthday, and a cake to make.

I wouldn't go out that day to fight grand Arthurian battles with Blaise, Andy, and Vincent. Instead, I stayed inside with the womenfolk, where the weapons were whisks and wooden spoons, and victory looked a lot like flour on your face and love hidden inside layers of cake.

By late afternoon, the cake was finished—frosted smooth, with "Happy Birthday, Vincent" written in perfect blue lettering like it belonged in a bakery window. The bus was swept, vacuumed, and strung with crinkled ribbon curling from the walls. His presents were stacked neatly on the table, and Mom's famous mini pizzas—golden, cheesy, and just slightly overbrowned on the edges—lined the counter like edible soldiers waiting for inspection.

We were ready. All we needed was the birthday boy.

No one ever really knew where anyone was; everyone was just "outside," which could mean anywhere within a mile radius. Mom handed me a task. "Go find Vincent and your missing siblings," she said, settling into her role as guardian of the goods.

I grabbed my bike, gave Heidi a pat on the head on my way out the door, pausing to think—"She looks bigger than yesterday; her appetite will likely be increasing, too." Shrugging it off, I continued with my mission.

"Bye, Mom." But her eyes were already closed, and she was napping.

The boys and I rolled up to the bus on our bikes, brakes squealing just in time to see Heidi bolt out the front door like a fugitive—with a pan flying after her.

"You damn dog!" Mom's voice echoed down the steps.

We dropped our bikes and raced inside. Mom stood in the middle of the bus, red-faced, holding an empty tray like a war widow clutching a folded flag.

"That dog jumped on the counter and ate *everything*—the pizzas, the cake, all of it!" she cried.

We froze, staring at the crime scene. Frosting smears on the cushion. A single pepperoni on the floor. The ribbon still swaying, festive and oblivious.

Dad came home not long after, and Mom launched into the saga with a tragic mix of fury and disbelief. I lingered nearby and caught bits of their quiet debate—something about eating out, budgets, birthdays, and the high cost of feeding both kids and canines.

Chapter Eight: One door closes, One door opens

We sat in silence, mourning the loss. Heidi, meanwhile, was under the bus licking icing off her nose, completely unapologetic.

Eventually, the verdict was in: it was a big expense, yes—but birthdays were sacred. No one would go without.

Mom went to the cupboard and pulled down her old Folgers coffee can, the one where she stashed her secret savings—coins, rolled bills, maybe a few crumpled fives tucked in for emergencies just like this.

We were called to load up the station wagon, which had been brought along for errands or emergencies—and birthday redemptions, apparently. First stop: the bakery, where a new cake was chosen by the birthday boy himself. Then on to the pizza parlor in town, where the smell of garlic and melted cheese seemed to erase all memory of the Great Heidi Heist.

It turned into a grand celebration. We laughed until we hiccupped, imagining that pudgy, well-fed dog inhaling trays of food like she was counting coup—racing the clock, beating Mom to the kitchen before she woke up. A crime of opportunity.

We stayed late, our eyes growing heavy under the soft lights of the restaurant, and then drove back to camp with full bellies and stories for a lifetime.

That night, I wrote in my commonplace book:

"Dogs are fun to have. Even when they're bad, they're still good."

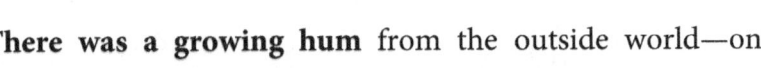

There was a growing hum from the outside world—one I could no longer ignore. Personal computers had arrived, and according to just about everyone, every household *needed* one. Books, like the whaling ships of old Nantucket, were said to be sailing off into obsolescence.

At the real estate office where I now worked as an agent, we technically had a computer. It sat in the corner like a piece of modern art while we carried on with our carbon paper, conference room handshakes, and folders—lots and lots of folders. But the whispers were getting louder: soon, all of it—paper, pens, physical files—would be relics of the past.

For a bookworm, this was an existential threat. I tried convincing myself it was just a fad, like disco or grapefruit diets. But the world didn't agree. Pressure mounted. People kept telling me how much easier my life would be.

This, I realized, was the beginning of something bigger—an accelerating shift, where technology would march ever deeper into the daily life of the common man, whether invited it or not. Resigning myself to the growing pressure to buy one, I slipped into my car, headed off to the store to buy one thinking, "Hmm. Well, we will see if it changes my life, but I am never buying one of those things called a Cell Phone."

The drive was pleasant enough. Autumn had returned to the Sierra Nevada's—my favorite time of year. It always felt like the world was finally exhaling after holding its breath through a long, hot summer. The sun was just beginning to peek through the thinning veil of gray clouds left behind by last night's mountain rain. I rolled down the windows to breathe it all in—the cool air, the damp earth, that fleeting scent of changing seasons.

Chapter Eight: One door closes, One door opens

The grass along the foothills had turned a lion-colored amber, soft and tired. The brilliant greens of summer were long gone, packed up like a memory.

In what felt like no time at all, the deed was done: I had bought a computer. Just like that. I turned the car around and headed home with this box—a strange, humming promise of the future—resting in my back seat.

Hours later, after much cable-wrangling and mild swearing, it stood assembled on the desk, blinking at me with quiet confidence. I sat down, took a deep breath, opened the instructional booklet, and began to read.

The booklet began with confidence—mine evaporated instantly.

"1 Byte
1024 Bytes = 1 Kilobyte
1024 Kilobytes = 1 Megabyte
1024 Megabytes = 1 Gigabyte
1024 Gigabytes = 1 Terabyte."

It went on to explain, with great enthusiasm, that everything in computers is binary. Storage capacities, it insisted, are all 2 to the Nth power. A kilobyte wasn't 1,000 bytes, oh no—it was 1,024, thank you very much. And a megabyte? 1,024 kilobytes, or 2 to the 20th power. Then came the big guns: a gigabyte, 2 to the 30th, which apparently equals 1,073,741,824 bytes.

I blinked at the page.

I hadn't even turned it yet and already felt like I was auditing a math class I didn't sign up for. So, this is what everyone meant by "it'll make your life easier."

I put the booklet down, and for the first time in ever in my life, I hated reading.

It was a Sunday morning when Dad woke me with a phone call—and some surprising news.

"Hey, guess what? Mom and I bought a new fifth wheel for the truck!"

Years ago, they had sold the old bus to a young family who tucked it away under an oak tree on their property. After that, they continued to travel, albeit much more compact now that all the kids were grown and gone. A beautiful new travel trailer instead of a refurbished bus worked well for them at this stage of their lives.

"Wait a minute," I said, "I thought you were never going to buy one of those new-fangled things, Dad?"

He chuckled. "Well, I only said that when you kids were little because I could never afford one."

I knew that was not entirely true. He loved building things and innovating. But his remark did make me wonder about all the times they might have made things sound better than they actually were so we would accept less.

The mechanic speak he had bequeathed to me as a child never left my mind. It made perfect sense why he purchased a fifth wheel and not a bumper pull trailer which becomes unstable during heavy winds. A fifth wheel offers more stability. And I did want to see it, so I called Little Andy up—who was not so little anymore—and we made arrangements to go see the new rig.

Chapter Eight: One door closes, One door opens

Pulling up to our parents' house, we spotted a gleaming new fifth-wheel trailer parked in the driveway. These days, they were hardly ever home—officially "snowbirds," which is just a polite way of saying traveling retired folks, chasing sunshine and cashing Social Security checks.

At the campgrounds, they even had clubs for the older nomads—bingo nights, potlucks, dancing, even perks for families homeschooling on the road.

Funny thing about being called a snowbird: suddenly, no one thinks you're eccentric. The moment something weird gets a label, it stops being weird—it becomes a lifestyle. Go figure.

I nudged Andy and said, "Can you believe it? Turns out we were unintentionally hip. Who knew?"

Dad walked us through the new rig, and it really was nice. We listened, oohhed and awwed at all the proper moments. After each fascinating fact—solar panels, leveling jacks, the backup camera with night vision—after highlighting each feature, he'd pause and look at us like a game show host waiting for applause.

Mom had some nice things stored in the cupboards, all held in place with little braces and brackets to keep them and watermelons from falling out on a sharp turn. Honestly, that was a pretty clever feature. She opened one cupboard with a flourish and said, "See? It doesn't even rattle."

As Dad wound his tour down, we all sat around the little kitchen table. Mom poured us each a cup of coffee—strong, hot, and served in real mugs, not travel ones. We started talking about the family. There were so many now it took some time to get through them all—wives, husbands, grandkids—and then Vincent.

Vincent, our priest in the family, had come down with pneumonia. "He's doing okay," Mom said, "but just okay." Andy and I both nodded, the coffee cooling in our hands.

When it was time to go, we stood outside in the driveway as the sky turned pink.

"Well, don't be strangers," Dad said, giving Andy a hearty slap on the back.

"Next time," Mom added, "bring me some of that granola I like from that co-op near your house."

"Okay," I said, hugging her.

The sun was just dipping below the trees as we pulled away. It was a good visit—one of those small, quiet reminders that nothing stays the same, which is both good and sad at the same time.

Logging onto my new computer that evening, I saw something that took my breath away: online college. I couldn't believe it. After all these years, a forgotten dream was suddenly within reach, a door that I thought was long closed, had suddenly opened.

Enrolling in classes was almost too easy. I signed up for English and Economics and began studying shortly after.

Economics turned out to be a little like psychology in disguise. When I came across the term *Creative Destruction*—meaning, essentially, to let something crappy fall apart so something better can take its place—I thought, "Well... I guess that pretty much sums up my marriage."

Week after week, I read voraciously and completed assignments like clockwork. Then, late one night, as the soft yellow glow of my lamp spilled across my homework, casting long shadows

Chapter Eight: One door closes, One door opens

over the pages, the sudden ring of the phone shattered the quiet—it was Dad.

It was strange to hear from him so soon after our most recent visit. I glanced at the clock: 11:16 p.m. My heart tightened. He never called this late unless something was wrong.

I hesitated, fingers hovering over the receiver, then braced myself and answered. His voice was heavy, trembling as he confirmed what I feared—Vincent had passed.

We didn't speak, just cried, the weight of loss hanging thick between us.

After a moment, Dad asked me to call Andy; he had others to notify. I dialed, and for hours we talked in low, broken whispers, holding each other steadily across the distance.

We talked on the phone for hours, swapping stories, laughing through tears until the sun nudged its way over the horizon. We relived that old bus and those croaking frogs, Marc's trumpet blaring, and Vincent with his folded underwear—always so meticulous, while the rest of us drove him nuts.

We agreed Vincent was born into the wrong family: neat and tidy, smart and pragmatic, a fine, detailed boy wedged between loudmouth mechanics and a beautiful Mom doing her best to hold it all together.

Driving to a funeral for your sibling is a heavy thing; as a kid before I knew what heartbreak felt like or why adults cried in parked cars, I thought the scariest thing in life was using the bathroom on a moving school bus, but now this took deeper processing. The complexities of identity, grief, forgiveness, and rebuilding are the things death forces you to think about. Turning each over and looking to see if there is anything that needs to be kept for the rest of the journey or cast out the window of a moving bus!

One thing was certain—people are what make the world fascinating and worth living. John Paul II said, "Man, created in the image and likeness of God, is the only creature whom God has willed for its own sake... and to whom God has entrusted the stewardship of creation."

And create we did, that bus filled with that crazy Italian Catholic family, spreading humor and love throughout the land.

The funeral was beautiful, the music was soul stirring, and the family and friends sat quietly as the priest read, from Psalms 34: 17-18, "The Lord hears his people when they call to him for help. He rescues them from all their troubles. The Lord is close to the brokenhearted; he rescues those whose spirits are crushed."

Then slowly, it was over. One by one we all got in our cars and drove our separate ways.

On the way home, I began to think of what some of the great Catholic authors thought about death,

* JRR Tolkien—'Human stories are practically always about one thing, aren't they? Death.'
* C.S Lewis—"God whispers to us in our pleasures, speaks in our conscience, but shouts in our pains: it is his megaphone to rouse a deaf world,"
* Bishop Fulton Sheen—"A happy death is a masterpiece, and no masterpiece was ever perfected in a day." Sheen added that people fear death chiefly because they "are not

Chapter Eight: One door closes, One door opens

prepared for it. Death is a beautiful thing for him who dies before he dies, by dying daily to the temptations of the world, the flesh, and the devil."

* Thomas Merton, reflected on the death of his own younger brother in, *The Seven Story Mountain*—"One thing I would say about my brother, John Paul: My most vivid memories of him, in our childhood, all fill me with poignant compunction at the thought of my own hard-heartedness, and his natural humility and love." ...

When someone passes, my family has a tradition of taking one thing they did and incorporating it into our own lives, so that they live on in some small way. The door is not completely shut; a new one opens in their memory. I thought about shaving my eyebrows to look like a Vulcan and then thought better of it. So, I went to the store instead and looked for a new iron to iron and care for my things better. I made a commitment to myself, to live more consciously, to care for what I had. I would fold my underwear, iron my handkerchiefs, and do things with just a little more attention to detail, as Vincent would have done. On my way out of the store, I saw a poster that had a little boy running down a country path with the words written over the top of it,

> *"Make the Child of your youth happy today:*
> *Go buy red licorice, take yourself to an amusement park all day, run just for the heck of it, sit and watch the ants, Choose the pizza, not the salad, and believe in God again."*

I bought the iron, the licorice, and the poster and went home to do my college homework, because after all these years, a forgotten dream was suddenly within reach.

"Light of Albion, guide my hand."

www.ingramcontent.com/pod-product-compliance
Lightning Source LLC
LaVergne TN
LVHW041333080426
835512LV00006B/430